All Stressed Up and No Place To Go

To Amber,
Laugh! Its
good medicine!
Lori Borgman

All
Stressed
Up and
No Place
To Go

Lori Borgman

emmis
books

For further information, contact the publisher at:

books

Emmis Books
1700 Madison Road
Cincinnati, OH 45206

www.emmisbooks.com

Library of Congress Cataloging-in-Publication Data

Borgman, Lori.
    All stressed up and no place to go / Lori Borgman.
        p. cm.
    ISBN 1-57860-214-9
    1. Family--Humor. [1. Family life--Humor.] I. Title.
    PN6231.F3B77 2005
    814'.6--dc22
                                    2004025025

Interior designed by Mary Barnes Clark
Edited by Jessica Yerega
Cover designed by Emily Schneider and Mary Barnes Clark
Illustrated by Adam Greber

Contents

PART 2:
YOU ALWAYS STRESS THE
ONES YOU LOVE

Introduction

I think we can all agree that stress is a terrible thing. It puts furrowed lines in your forehead and tension in your marriage. It elevates your blood pressure and makes you say crazy things like, "Charge it. The Visa bill can't be that big yet."

I think we can also agree on this: Stress is as unavoidable as death and taxes. At least for most of us. Oh sure, once in a blue moon you read about some ancient recluse emerging from a cave deep in the jungle and asking if World War II has ended. The old guy looks a little rough around the edges, but when you consider that he has lived decades without cable television, the Internet, and frequent flyer miles, you realize he may be living one of the most stress-free lives on the entire planet. The more you study him, the more you envy his carefree and simple lifestyle. Momentarily, in the light of screaming babies, hormonal teenagers, and an automobile mechanic who has left the brief message, "Seven-hundred-dollar minimum," it is a way of life that looks extremely attractive.

Of course, looking through rose-colored glasses, you neglect to factor in a few minor irritations that accompany such a back-to-the-basics and natural lifestyle—eating insects three times a day, bats tangled in matted hair, and chronic scurvy. It is probably safe to say that, rather than fleeing stress and heading to the hills, most of us would rather stay and confront it head on.

That is precisely what this book does. It confronts stress. Unfortunately, this book will not help you win the battle with stress. Why not? Because that is impossible. Contrary to the popular bumper sticker, trees are *not* America's most renewable resource. Stress is. There's no getting away from it. Stress is like crabgrass and middle-age spread. You may tame it for a season, but sooner or later it sneaks right back up on you.

So even though this book probably won't remove the crow's feet around your eyes, fix your kid's overbite, or organize your sock drawer for the next six months, you should still read it. Why? Because this book might make you laugh at someone you know—yourself. And sometimes, a little laughter may be the only thing standing between you and a bed in a quiet little institution in the country.

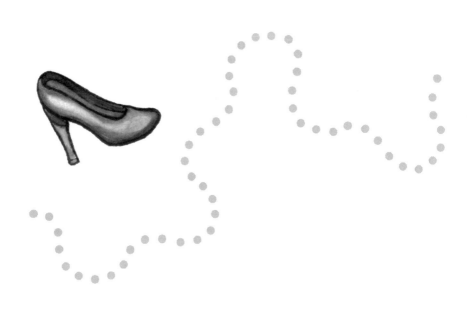

part 1 :

Got Stress?

1

In the Beginning

S tress is nothing new. Of course, we baby boomers think we are the first ones to experience it, just like we think we are the first ones to experience parenting woes, job stress, and rapid hair loss. Actually, stress has existed since the beginning of the world. The origin of stress can be traced back to a state-of-the-art laboratory known as the Garden of Eden. The Garden of Eden, with its babbling brooks and winding paths, lush vegetation, and a vast array of exotic wildlife, was idyllic. Paradise, even. Adam and the animals feasted on the succulent fruits and plump vegetables. They savored lingering sunsets, leisurely walked in the cool of the evening, and stared open-mouth at constellations blazing in the midnight sky. Life was easy and the living was good. Then, one day, God created Eve.

Enter stress, stage left.

Life in the Garden began to change. It seemed to Adam that the brooks weren't the only thing babbling now. He hated to say anything (and he really *couldn't* say anything, even if he wanted to, since it was nearly impossible to get a word in), but it seemed to him as though Eve talked a bit much. He awoke to the sound of her voice describing the weather and announcing the day's plans. He listened while she narrated the day's events as they unfolded before them. He found it amazing that she could still find something to talk about as they ate their last fried plantains of the day. Even when he was stretched out for the night on spongy palm leaves, with his head nestled on his favorite Border collie, drifting off to sleep, her voice filled the air, chatting on and on about emotions and feelings, relationships and issues, things Adam knew absolutely nothing about before her arrival.

It wasn't just her talking. It was her restless spirit. She was never content with things the way they were, always making major changes and minor adjustments. Or rather telling *him* to.

"Move the bamboo shoots to the side of the variegated hostas. Good. Now move the basil a little farther away from the oregano," she'd instruct. "That's it, that's it. No, no, no, just a goat's width closer to rhodies. Back to the left a bit. There you go. No, no, over just a little bit closer to that juniper."

If she wasn't asking him to move something, she was asking him to make something. "Adam, we need one flat oblong rock to set close to the fire and two smaller, rounder ones on which to prop our feet. And I don't want sandstone. I can't stand the way it crumbles and tracks into the cave. I'm thinking something in a marble or limestone would be nice. Could you do that? Soon? This afternoon, maybe? What do you think?"

What did he think? He thought he had gotten by quite nicely squatting on the ground next to the fire. But no, squatting would not do for Eve—she was creating something cozy and comfortable, something color-coordinated and called a conversation pit. Adam could only hope a conversation pit meant a deep, deep hole he could enter to escape the constant stream of words.

Adam wasn't the only one who had some adjusting to do. Eve thought it strange the way Adam could go mornings and afternoons without talking at all. She'd start a conversation and he'd just grunt. "Oh." "Huh." "Really." Eve suspected maybe Adam had been with the animals too long and wasn't comfortable talking to another human being. Maybe he needed her to show him how it was done. She had so much to show him: How to pick up his walking sticks so they weren't lying out where anybody could trip over them. How to sleep on his side so he didn't snore so loudly. How to eat without his elbows so high in the air that the parrots perched on them. How to cover the pit toilet after he had used it.

Adam had a few other habits that Eve found most peculiar. She didn't know why, but it nagged at her the way he'd round up a dozen chimps and they'd bat that silly coconut around with a small, straight branch from an ash tree for hours on end. It was almost as ridiculous as when he'd waste autumn afternoons in the meadowland with the jungle's largest gorillas, throwing an eggplant back and forth. Of course, they didn't always throw it. Sometimes one of them would hold it in place on the ground while another one would charge at it full-speed and give it a powerful kick. Other times, one of them would just snatch it up, hold it close to its chest and run like crazy. Why they enjoyed all that running, grunting, and diving for an eggplant was beyond Eve. There was a glorious profusion of eggplant in the garden. Why in the name of all that is natural,

Eve wondered, did they find it necessary to bloody noses and bruise ribs for just one?

As a couple, Adam and Eve had their minor differences, what we in today's sophisticated and modern world would call small stresses. Nothing major, just trivial irritations, small annoyances, a phrase or a look misinterpreted now and then. It was nothing explosive or devastating, but more like an occasional low and gentle rumble heard in the distance.

No, explosive came the day the stress level hit 8.7 on the Richter Scale, when two certain someones broke the only teeny-weeny rule in Paradise. Who knows why it happened, really. Stress from the new environment, tension in the relationship, the need for assertion, unresolved issues, a cry for attention. The rule was not to eat from the Tree of Good and Evil, and eat they did. The ensuing events can only be described as a very nasty round of "He Said, She Said."

He said she made him do it. She said the serpent made her do it. And so it went. He said, she said, he said, she said, until God said, "OUT!" They were banished from Paradise.

Stress mushroomed. Far from their lovely starter home in Paradise, Adam and Eve now rose before the sun and ran with the speed of jaguars struggling to juggle work and family, hunting and gathering, cleaning the cave and building fires. In what little spare time they had, they staved off hostile neighbors and tried to involve the kids in a broad range of community league sports. Soon they found themselves spread too thin. Stress began manifesting itself in dull headaches, muscle spasms, a harsh edge to their voices, and, "No honey, not tonight." Sometimes the tension was so thick you could swing a club at it. Adam and Eve were awash in stress. They had fallen into a pattern of living that would set the standard for generations to come. The rest, as they say, is history.

2

Tense: Past and Present

A fascinating sidelight within the continually evolving history of stress is the very word itself. As far as I can remember, and my kids will tell you that covers the Byzantine Empire, the Iron Age, and the Age of Disco, the word *stress* is relatively new. We just think it is old because we hear it 937 bazillion times each day.

But the fact is, until just a few decades ago, the word most commonly used to describe the feeling that you are about to jump out of your skin was *nervous*. As in, "Don't bang the porch swing into the house; it makes your grandma *nervous*." Or, "Don't kick the back of your father's seat when he's driving; it makes him *nervous*."

I miss the word nervous. It had an edge to it that the word stress simply does not possess. The word stress is so overworked that it has become dull and blase. We use it as a noun (Stress: Ten Non-Fat Ways to Tame It), a verb ("All this talk of erotic body piercing is stressing me out"), and even as an adjective ("Those bags under her eyes are the size the Pony Express used to carry. Wow, is she stressed!"). Not only do *people* feel stress, but even inanimate objects are soaking it up.

A friend recently invited me to look at the screened-in porch her husband had built over the summer. She pointed out its many fine features, including a grooved-tongue floor, vaulted ceiling, and beautiful southern exposure. "It's all made of stressed ash," she said. I'd always thought of a screened-in porch as a happy, restful place where you could lounge with a book and feel a gentle breeze tickle your skin. I had no idea stress was now infecting wood. But in these days when our minds are stressed, our bodies are stressed, our relationships are stressed, and even our plants and pets are stressed, anything is possible.

Even our physical injuries are riding the stress bandwagon. We used to break bones or fracture them. Today, our bones suffer stress fractures. It is hard to say what the advantage of a stress fracture is over, say, a hairline fracture. Unless, of course, due to the stress component, one is offered an anti-depressant to accompany the pain killer. Then there may well be a measurable benefit to having a stress fracture as opposed to an old-fashioned break.

Stress is so overused, it has become the Rodney Dangerfield of words. It just can't get no respect. Stress has been mass-produced in such mammoth quantities that it has become common and ordinary—like cheap white bread that sticks to the roof of your mouth. The word nervous, on the other hand, has class—a certain chic about it, if you will. Stress is to gummy white bread, what nervous is to a fine French baguette with a crusty exterior and chewy interior.

For the most part, we know exactly what to expect when people announce that they are experiencing stress. They will get a little crabby and thin-skinned and snap someone's head off. On the other hand, nervous has an aura of mystique and unpredictability. Whenever I was told as a child (usually at a Sunday family gathering with seventeen first cousins, doors slamming and babies wailing), that an aunt or grandma was getting nervous, I was never certain of what to expect. Nervous had a dark and ominous dimension to it. Perhaps the term carried greater weight because it was often backed up with a small, but impressive, demonstration for those yet unconvinced.

"You don't believe your (choose one) aunt, mother, grandmother, is nervous? Look at her hands shake."

The nervous woman in question would then respond on cue, raise her hand for spectators to observe an ever so slight, yet discernable trembling. I always bought it as a kid and scrambled to the farthest opposite corner—away from the knives. Today, as a mother who is frequently brought to the brink of nervousness, I suspect that a fair share of those demonstrations were for effect. It was a way to get the kids out of the kitchen so adults could resume talk too rich for our unripened ears.

When I took the risk of hanging around to see what a full-blown case of nervous looked like, the ensuing events never lived up to my expectations. The nervous person would usually get up from the table and pour herself another cup of coffee. Strong, thick, black coffee, which probably accounted for the shakiness far more than being nervous did.

Much to my disappointment, the fireworks and drama the word nervous conjured up never materialized. Nobody's eyes bulged out of their heads. Nor did their skin erupt with a hideous purple rash. Not once did my mother lose control, rip the sleeves off her dress, and begin pulling out her hair. Nor did my grandmother ever go berserk, as I pictured she might. Not once did she charge out onto the porch, where we were banging the swing into the house, and wrap that heavy porch swing chain around some scrawny kid's neck. Nor did my father, whom my mother said my brother and I made nervous by fighting in the car, ever jerk the car to a screeching halt, rip us out of the back seat, and say, "That's enough. Here's the water jug. You two can *walk* to Wichita!"

It never happened, none of it. But the point is, the mere mention of the word nervous made us think it might. What did happened was this: Someone would get a little crabby and thin-skinned and snap somebody's head off.

At its core, nervous is almost identical to stress: a state of being denoted by tension, jumpiness, crabbiness, and being easily excited and overly agitated. Nervous just has the ability to clear a room faster. Which is why I hope the word nervous will one day return to our everyday vernacular.

In the meantime, I'll be on the front porch perfecting my shaky hand move.

3

The Eight-Minute
Meltdown

The things that stress a woman usually aren't major
things. They are small things.

It is the steady accumulation of small irritations that
cause women to develop facial tics and curl up under the
bed in the fetal position repeating the Greek alphabet
backward. It is walking into church and having one of
your kids ask if you have any Q-tips in your purse. It is
having a kid hand you a stopwatch and ask if you'll time
her while she belches her ABCs.

Mothers do not lose their grip on reality over a child's
science grade that could have been better. The front door left
open overnight is disconcerting, but by itself is insufficient to
send any woman to a padded cell. What pushes women over
the edge is the steady drip of small annoyances. It is that
gradual buildup of tiny unpredictable aggravations that
can propel a woman from competent to crazy in under
ten minutes.

Consider the following:

At 7:00 A.M., Mom is in the kitchen where sunshine is
pouring into the kitchen through an open window. Raisins

are cheerfully line-dancing in perfect synchronization with bran flakes on the counter. All is well with the world. Until 7:01.

At 7:01, the morning cereal selection is pronounced unsatisfactory by a child who awoke in a wrong-side-of-the-bed, pit bull sort of mood. At 7:02, the surly child scorning the cereal is temporarily banished from the kitchen and exiled into the family room.

Seconds later, another child who has wandered into the kitchen spots a huge, disgusting fly on the wall. An older male sibling rounds the corner and proudly announces he will kill the fly by zapping it with a rubber band.

Those hoping for a civilized bite to eat before departing for the day, and yet uncertain of the ricochet effect of death by rubber band, grab cereal bowls and boxes and dash to the opposite side of the kitchen.

It is now 7:03. Mom, who only minutes ago came downstairs in a peaceful, Julie Andrews-*Sound-of-Music*-in-love-with-life kind of mood, is now yelling. Loudly. She is hollering at son not to attempt to kill fly with a rubber band. "What kind of moron kills insects with rubber bands?" Mom sounds neither peaceful nor serene, but agitated. Extremely agitated. Strait-jacket agitated.

The commotion escalates at 7:04 as Dad joins the fracas, demanding son use a traditional fly swatter. Son dismisses the suggestion, stating that the rubber band way is the best way to kill a fly. Dad storms to garage in pursuit of the fly swatter to demonstrate the proper method of exterminating flies.

7:05: After considerable thrashing about in the garage, unable to find a fly swatter, Dad returns from garage with a furrowed brow and extra large straw broom and readies himself to take aim.

7:06: Mother lodges vehement, emotional protest and is completely ignored. Despite heartfelt pleas, Dad swings broom in vicinity of fly parked adjacent to an oak plate rack, which cradles family heirlooms, including babies' first mugs.

SWOOSH!

WHACK!

Fly continues to grip wall, but is obviously stunned. He slowly turns his little head toward these evil, early morning predators, sticks out his tongue, and makes a rude motor-boat sound as he darts over to the corner windowsill.

7:07: Son, seizing what may be his last opportunity, pulls back on green rubber band, takes aim, releases and . . .

PHHHHHT!

The fly has been zapped. Direct hit; first try.

Meanwhile, hungry child with a flair for drama, previously exiled to the family room, resumes begging for toast. A heel? A crust? Perhaps a handful of crumbs from beneath the toaster? Hearing no rapid shuffling of feet to accommodate her request, child predicts she will collapse before 9 A.M. and warns that the school nurse probably will be contacting a social worker.

7:08: Middle child goes ballistic. Not only is she having a bad hair day, but she has discovered the monster fly has disemboweled upon impact, scattering bloody fly innards hither and yon upon the white kitchen floor. Child with unruly bangs and no stomach for blood screams that she is going to lose her toast.

7:09: Did someone say *toast*? Exiled child resumes howling for breakfast. Please, please. Can't anyone else hear her stomach growling? They can probably hear it growling down at Children's Services Division, she wails.

Mom, who only moments ago was bubbly and perky, now has a white-knuckle grip on the kitchen sink. Her nostrils are flared. Her breathing is shallow. Her eyes have narrowed to frightening slits due to a mushrooming tension headache. Bubbly and perky are ancient history.

What we have witnessed here is the anatomy of a classic meltdown. In merely eight minutes, a rational, calm, self-possessed woman has been rendered a near nut case by nothing more than the annoying, irritating, and inconsequential.

It's nothing big; it's everything small.

Some days, it's life.

4

Fright or Flight?

M y heart began beating wildly as soon as I heard the man say, "Excuse me, ma'am, I'm a plain clothes security officer for the store and I'm going to have to ask you to take those off."

Shallow breathing. Sweaty palms. Elevated blood pressure. Tightened muscles. This is what stress does to the human body. The brain receives a panic note (in this case, a strange man, wearing four-days beard growth and a plaid flannel shirt, standing eight inches from my face). The fear signal is instantly forwarded to the adrenal glands perched in ready position atop the kidneys. Working on cue, the stress hormone floodgates spring open wide and adrenalin gushes into the blood stream, putting all physical systems on red alert.

I looked at the security officer and manage the verbal strength to squeak out a "Pardon me?"

"The in-line skates," he said. "Please take them off. I know you're just trying them on, but I've been watching you and I think you're a liability. These floors are slick and I'm concerned you won't be able to stop before hitting the coffee makers."

Thanks, bud, I think you look pretty graceful yourself.

Okay, fine. I sit down, begin wrestling off the skates, and at the same time give my body a chance to recover. Gradually, my heartbeat returns to normal and I'm no longer on the verge of hyperventilating. The adrenalin surge has subsided.

I was shopping with my friend Mary who had duped me into believing that the two of us should purchase in-line skates and launch a new fitness routine. Mary's plan was that in-line skating would keep us in shape—such as our shapes were—improve our health, and reduce our stress levels.

I had covered no more than five linear feet in the skates and, instead of averting stress, they were already causing stress. Not a good sign for a new fitness program. As for the thinly disguised accusation from the plain clothes officer that I was a klutz on wheels, for the record, it was the first time I had ever been on rollerblades. And furthermore, I certainly *would* have been able to stop before hitting the coffee makers. There was a lovely display of toasters and bread machines that I would have taken out first. His precious little coffee makers would have been perfectly safe.

Rollerblading with Mary was the first time I truly came to a clear understanding of the physiology of stress. There were the little stresses when Mary would skate backward or spin in circles and say that anybody could do it. Of course, that was if "anybody" had the guts to try. This was low-level stress, heart flutters, and mild anxiousness. Then there was moderate level stress—irritation, crabbiness, defensiveness—when Mary suggested that we try sailing down Claridge Road. This is a street in our otherwise flat subdivision so steep that even four-wheel drive SUVs pause, shudder, and think twice before descending.

I pointed this out to Mary, and she pointed out that I shouldn't worry about accidents and injury because she was a professionally trained member of the medical community. While this was true, I pointed out that she was an obstetrics/gynecology nurse who worked in a neonatal unit at a women's hospital. Not only was I not pregnant, the injuries we were apt to incur rollerblading were far more likely to be to our arms, legs, and skulls as opposed to the birth canal. I could just picture it. I would foolishly take the challenge to do suicide hill, wipe out halfway down, roll in a wild out-of-control somersault fashion, and land at the base of the hill in a mangled heap. As I lie there with bone shards protruding from my legs and compound fractures in both wrists, Mary would charge at me with one of those ultrasound dopplers and ask how close together my contractions were.

Eventually, the number of streets in the neighborhood that were smooth enough for us amateurs to skate on shrank to two. Mary and I switched to walking for our fitness program. At least Mary called it walking; I always felt we were running. My survival strategy was to tap her hot spot—international politics and foreign affairs (she hails from a big military family)—before we tackled Heart Attack Hill. When Mary became worked up about foreign policy, she would become slightly winded, giving me a chance to catch up and slow the pace.

The walking phase of our fitness and stress-reduction program was where we met the big kahuna of adrenalin rushes.

We are walking along, according to schedule, approaching the hill and beginning a heated discussion about North Korea. A dog barks in the distance. Ten paces later, the dog comes tearing out of the brush and into view. It is a large hunting dog. Given the distinct absence of any duck or water fowl, the natural conclusion is that we are the hunted. The dog is standing and barking and looking in our direction. For a brief second, we freeze. The dog barks with greater intensity, spins his back legs, and begins running hard in our direction. He is neither behind a fence nor on a leash.

The hypothalamus in the brain has sounded the mother of all panic alarms to the adrenal gland in the kidney region. Adrenalin begins surging through the body. My heartbeat dips six floors south and then rockets skyward. My hair follicles stand on end and, for a flash, I feel a passing wave of nausea. Or was it my calf being ripped open? No, it was only nausea.

This is the human body in full stress alert. This is also the human body confronted with the age-old question of fight or flight? Fight is out of the question as this dog has two large advantages—sparkling white canines, one on the left, one on the right.

Mary has the same instinctive reaction. Flight. Which is why she jumps to the other side of me. And I jump to the other side of her. And she jumps to the other side of me. Like two checkers making their way across a red and black board, we are simultaneously fleeing and hopping to the other side of each other in hopes of avoiding the dog's powerful jaw. Look, I never said this was a story about friendship and sacrifice. This is a story about stress hormones, a big dog with sharp teeth, and the hope of survival.

Legs that moments ago had been weak and tired are now fully charged and ready to attempt a three-minute mile. Suddenly, the dog comes to an abrupt halt. He is still barking furiously, but for some peculiar reason has stopped at the corner of the lot. Looking back to make sure he's stopped, I notice a little green tag protruding from the ground. Invisible fencing. That dog has experienced a few stress hormones of his own. He has been trained that if he crosses the lot line, he will be zapped with a small surge of electricity. Being a smart puppy, he has learned from experience that it is better to stop than to be scorched.

Stress hormones turn off and on like the faucet on a tub. Sometimes they blast through in great quantities. Other times they come intermittently, or in a trickle. The problem is that the faucet is turned on frequently these days, not just in the face of plain clothes security officers or aggressive dogs. Stress hormones routinely seep out during traffic jams, fifteen-minute waits at the grocery express line, pressure on the job, looming deadlines, and nights spent waiting up for teenagers who have missed their curfews.

Researchers agree that chronic stress can increase the risk of heart attack and may even clog arteries the same way eating an entire cherry cheesecake would. They also agree that regular exercise is still one of the best weapons for fighting stress.

I suppose that's good advice, as long as the stress from the exercise doesn't kill you first.

5

Tae Bo or Not
Tae Bo

If you want to test your threshold of stress, try out the
new feature on the Lands' End Web site called My
Personal Model. You can enter your measurements, select
clothes, and then watch as they appear on a computer-
generated model exactly your shape and size.

I thought it would be fun to try My Personal Model, so
I pulled the shades, closed the drapes, and bolted the door.
Then, I entered my measurements into the appropriate
categories, hit "enter"—and watched the computer crash.

I took ten deep breaths and did the only thing a devas-
tated woman could. I rebooted the computer and entered
Cindy Crawford's measurements. (By the way, Cindy, you
should be receiving a casual chic funnelneck sweater and
pleated gabardine trousers in three to four working days.
They look great on you. I hope you like navy.)

The computer model fiasco was so traumatic it left me
vulnerable to a host of temptations: dieting, counting
calories, drinking eight glasses of water a day, and—the
ultimate enticement—Tae Bo. Tae Bo is an aerobic exercise
program copyrighted by martial arts expert Billy Blanks,

who has biceps the size of watermelons and is kick-boxing his way to the bank with his successful video series. Tae Bo blends tae kwon do, boxing, music, and a dozen good-looking Californians in exercise outfits so skintight they must be removed after the workout session by a technician certified to operate the Jaws of Life.

After only several weeks of doing Tae Bo, I have experienced dramatic results. My right shoulder double clicks when I move my arm in a circle, and both knees begin twitching every morning around 2 A.M. I might have lost an inch or two from my waist, but that could change by the time this sees print, whereas the shoulder and knee spasms will no doubt stay with me for months.

My daughters, who have done Tae Bo for a year, say I injured myself because I didn't use proper technique. Sure, blame the mother.

Sometimes I do Tae Bo with my daughters, but I prefer doing it alone, as the girls are so critical.

"Mom, you can't do Tae Bo sitting on the couch."

"Well, I can do some of it, and some movement is better than none."

"Mom, why is there white chocolate on your fingers?"

"Hey, girls, we can't all just hang out, pampering ourselves doing exercise videos. Some of us have to work. Some of us even have to dip pretzels from time to time."

My main problem doing Tae Bo is that I start thinking that I look like the gals in the video. Thin gals. Sometimes, I so identify with the gals in the video that I even think I'm blonde. When I think I'm thin, I'm prone to eat, which leaves me anything but thin. When I think I'm blonde, I have the urge to buy a convertible, which is not nearly as fattening as thinking I'm thin, although a lot harder to explain to the husband.

My other concern about Tae Bo is that many of the gals in the video have rippled indentations beneath their ribs. At first, I thought these were surgical scars, but my girls say it is a muscle set in the abdomen known as a six-pack. My mother says forget it, there has never been a woman in our family to carry a six-pack. We are all genetically predisposed to carry a full case—of Slim-Fast.

Oh well, I'm still at it. Billy Blanks is on the screen shouting at me to, "Push yourself! Reach inside for your higher power!" My body may be in front of the video, but my higher power has taken off for frozen yogurt with hot fudge and toasted pecans. In a convertible.

6

Scentually Yours

You probably have a Dollars for Scents store at your mall, too. Ours is nestled between Victoria's Not So Very Secret and the Long and Leggy Lady shop. It is the trendiest spot in the city. Shoppers flock to the store in droves, gleefully plunking down cash and credit cards for bottles, tubes, and jars of all-natural oils and herbs that promise to cure what ails them—namely, stress.

Dollars for Scents is an olfactory wonder of the world. It is also a friendly-looking little store with bubbly, young clerks who look about fourteen years old. According to their driver's licenses, they are really in their late twenties, but with all those rejuvenating potions at their disposal, they are turning back the hands of time.

Soft rock music plays in the background, and row after row of lotions, gels, and candles glisten under the gleam of track lighting. Each and every bottle is guaranteed to make you a relaxed person . . . an invigorated person . . . a poised person . . . an energetic person . . . a mellow person. Yes, these scented lotions and gels will make you a completely different person, nothing at all like the person you really are!

There are leg lotions able to revive calves, face creams to erase crow's-feet, foot creams to massage toes and heels, candles to put your sweetie in the mood, and shampoos that will even help your hair happy up and swing.

The store is absolutely permeated with fragrance. By pointing my nose in the direction of the cash register, I can catch a whiff of rose water. By directing my schnoz toward the door, I pick up the scent of sandalwood. Every which way you turn, a new and relaxing aroma seeps into your nasal passages—waaaay up your nasal passages. The store is so saturated with scents that during my first visit there, I find myself scanning the back wall looking for emergency gas masks next to the fire extinguisher. Alarmed that there are none, I turn to leave when a sales clerk, wearing a stretchy black dress two sizes too tiny for her hiney, approaches me and whispers, "Welcome to the world of aromatherapy. Would you like to sample our Stress Relief Spray?"

"What is it?" I ask.

"It's just the thing. All-natural, of course," she hisses, tossing back her all natural highlighted hair. "It contains clary sage and basil oils that relieve stress. Use it at night. Mist it all over your night clothes, your pillows, and your sheets. You'll be *amazed* at what it does for your stress."

"But my night clothes, pillows, and sheets don't cause me stress," I say. "It's usually that body sleeping in the other half of the bed that causes me stress."

"Spritz him, too," she purrs.

"Great, I'll take two."

She looks me up and down, then straight in the eye and whispers, "Perhaps a little aphrodisiac might help?"

"Oh no, my hair's always this frizzy when it's humid," I say.

"No, no," she giggles again. "An aphrodisiac contains rose oil and patchouli oil. It promotes openness and honesty. The scent brings out affection, charm, and closeness."

I nearly swoon just listening to her describe such soothing and relaxing powers. I near a trance-like state when I hear her say, "The added sandalwood and ylang ylang help promote sensuality, inspire affection, and give you an insatiable lust for closeness."

Her last claim jolts me to my senses. "For twenty-one years, I've been struggling to find ways to keep romance in my marriage, and now you tell me they sell it in a two-ounce bottle?"

"That's right," she says with a nod. "It virtually ignites a room."

"Is it legal?" I ask.

"Between consenting adults," she purrs, with a wink.

"I'll take five."

We continue our tour, resting briefly by a wooden basket full of miniature samples. "You might also like to try this special pulse-point lotion blending peppermint, eucalyptus, and rosemary," she says. "It can ease mental fatigue, improve memory, and help you think more clearly."

"With powers like that, why just smell it?" I say. "With stress like mine, maybe I should drink it and get it into my system faster."

"I think not," she says with a raised eyebrow. It is the look of a first grade teacher on lunch room duty, glaring at a kid blowing bubbles in his milk carton. "If you're feeling a bit harried, we have a lovely lemon balm good for soothing tension."

"As soothing as lemon poppy seed cake?" I inquire with a snicker.

The teacher look, again.

We saunter over to a display featuring a relaxing and mystical gel potpourri guaranteed to make brain waves more shallow.

"And that's a good thing?" I ask.

The clerk tilts her nose into the air and says, "Why, it was used as a healing balm for years by the Egyptians and Romans."

Yeah, I think to myself. And look what shallow brain waves did for them: dry skin from overexposure to the sun, followed by death.

The clerk then takes me to a special nook where aromatherapy devotees can custom design their own products. "By mixing a few drops of oil, another few drops of a complementary but not competing oil, and pouring them into a spray bottle filled with a 3:1 mineral water, distilled water solution—"

"Thank, but no thanks," I say. "I'll make my own room freshener the day I start beating out my laundry on rocks down by the river."

A little discouraged by my resistance, she spritzes herself with a store sample of fir and bayberry blend, called Piney Woods Energizer, and suggests that perhaps we should peruse the high-tech end of aromatherapy—a Nature's Aroma combination CD player, alarm clock, and egg timer.

"This features two electric aromatherapy diffusers that permeate the room with the fragrance of your choice," she explains.

"Do you have the smell of chocolate chip cookies baking? I love that smell," I say.

"No," she answers curtly.

"Then how about the smell of hot coffee?"

"How about trying Starbucks?"she retorts.

I listen passively as she explains the three sound-conditioning tracks that feature babbling brook, tropical jungle, and gentle rain.

"That's great," I say. "Do they have a track on there that plays a vacuum running? If there's anything that makes me feel refreshed, it's the sound of someone else cleaning the house."

No response.

"Okay then, do they have a sound track of water noises in the bathroom? You know, sink noises, the toilet flushing, the shower running. I love hearing those sounds when I'm still in bed. Makes me feel like I'm on borrowed time. Someone else is up and at the grind, and I'm still in bed in the sleep position."

No response, again.

She concludes the Nature's Aroma CD player and clock demonstration by pointing out the three stress-relieving alarm options: chimes, handbells, or dulcimer.

Eventually, we cover the entire store, fanning, spritzing, oiling, sniffing, and dabbing our way through an endless blend of bergamot, orange, and chamomile. By the end of the tour, I am a convert. I believe in the stress-relieving powers of creme caramel, blueberry bliss, and turquoise oceans. Not only am I a believer, I am casting off stress the way a snake sheds skin. I have succumbed to the powers of aromatherapy. Either that, or I am nearing unconsciousness from the allergic reaction to all the heavily fragranced gels, lotions, creams, and candles. In any case, I feel such a deep sense of peace and calm that I wonder if I have the adrenalin needed to drive home.

They say you can never put a price tag on good health. But personal check number 4807, written to Dollars for Scents, would indicate that mine came to roughly $135.95 (tax included).

7

Down the Drain

Not long after my visit to Dollars for Scents, I happened on one of those home and garden shows that featured a professional perfectionist touting the therapeutic value of a relaxing bath. "Reduce stress," she said. "Ease muscle tension," she said. "Soothe away your cares," she said. "Wash your worries down the drain," she said. For a minute, I almost believed her.

Then, I flashed back to the last time I actually tried a long soak in the tub to reduce stress. After sixty seconds in the bubbles, there was a commotion on the other side of the door that sounded like two World Wrestling Entertainment maniacs ripping each other's heads off.

"What's going on out there?" I yelled, tension filling every muscle in my neck.

"Nothing!"

"It sounds like something to me. It sounds like war!" I shouted.

Wild laughter.

"Naw, we're just doing a scene from *Fight Club*."

Fight Club, a movie about boxing, is in their repertoire;

The Sound of Music is not.

Thirty seconds later, there was a knock on the bathroom door.

"Occupado!" I hollered.

"I need in."

"I gave at the office," I said.

"I need my hairbrush."

"Not now," I yelled, "I'm relaxing! Besides, the door is locked."

"No problem. I'll just straighten a paper clip and I can have the door open in thirty seconds."

Ten seconds after that, the phone rang. It was for me. Like that was a surprise.

Thirty seconds after that, there was another knock on the bathroom door.

"What *now*?" I yelled.

"UPS, ma'am. I need a signature."

I wondered if this gal on television—who rolls her own oats and plucks her own geese to make her own down pillows—ever put her luxury bath to the test by slipping into the suds against a backdrop of scenes from *Fight Club*, threats of an intruder picking the lock with a paper clip, and a package delivery.

I realized that, these days, my main problem with a luxury bath is getting access to the tub. My, how times have changed. When the kids were little, I had to threaten them to get them into the bathroom. Now that they are teenagers, I have to threaten them to get them to come out.

When they were infants, they had no say in the matter. The bathroom was the hub of their very existence. This is where I would change them, hose them, suds them, dip them, rinse them, powder them, and pray that the sweet, baby fresh clean smell would last for at least five minutes before I was forced to repeat the process again.

As toddlers, I would lure them into the bathroom by hiding a wind-up music box that played "Lara's Theme" from *Doctor Zhivago*. I promised the music would play again if they would sit on the special potty chair and do their business. I would perch on the side of the tub, run a steady trickle of water, and describe the beauty of Niagara Falls, waiting and hoping for a miracle. The potty chair they hated; the bathtub they loved.

Why not? The tub was a trip to the pool without the constraint of swimsuits. It was a cross between Toys "R" Us in a flash flood and a water park with squirt guns, empty dishsoap bottles, soap crayons, and a fleet of rubber ducks. The kids splashed, fished, swam, and snorkeled until their little bodies shriveled like raisins.

By the time they hit elementary school, the tub lost its appeal. Our oldest was known to fill the tub and spend twenty minutes slapping a wet washcloth against the tile wall without so much as getting his big toe wet. He would come out with the same grungy clothes on, the same dirt still crusted on his neck, the same grime stuck behind his ears, and say, "Whuddyamean?" when I'd say, "Okay, now get back in there and wash!" A mother may not be able to see through a bathroom door, but she can sure hear.

At the onset of adolescence, their relationship with the bathroom changed. At different times, each one of the three walked into the bathroom, closed the door, and has not been seen since. Each and every day, I stand on the other side of the door waiting and hoping for a life form to emerge.

I hear drawers peeling open and slamming shut like my

offspring are in there conducting a bathroom vanity durability test for *Consumer Reports.* Sliding mirrors on the front of the medicine cabinets glide back and forth and back and forth until it sounds like the entire Ice Capades troupe practicing before the big performance. Blow dryers run for so long you'd think someone was defrosting a frozen hippo.

But the greatest mystery of all is the thirty-minute shower. The habitual offender is a kid who plastered Save the Earth decals on a notebook in middle school and goaded us into paying for curbside recycling.

I tried placing a timer in the bathroom and setting a five-minute shower limit. Three months later, the timer rusted. I've tried pounding on the door, heaping heavy guilt, and employed underhanded manipulation tactics, all for naught.

As a last resort, I have stooped to terror:

"You've got one minute before I go behind a little door of my own."

My little door is the one at the back of the hallway linen closet that opens to hot and cold water valves. One 360-degree twist and the hot water immediately stops.

Once in a while, stress forces us all to play a little dirty.

Livin' La Cell Phone Vida

In yet another step to reduce stress and further simplify our lives, we are now the proud owners of a third cordless phone (with twenty-five channels and ten speed-dial memory keys).

An appliance manufacturer recently announced plans for a new microwave oven that will cook the food for you. You just scan the package and the microwave does the rest. There is also a Lincoln Continental in the works that will read e-mail messages to you while you drive. Once they combine those two simple ideas, they'll really have a sure money maker.

One day soon, you'll see a mother zipping down the interstate at seventy-five miles per hour with a cell phone attached to one ear and her fingers hammering at her dashboard e-mail program when arms and legs start flying in the back seat, and she'll be yelling, "Would you kids knock that off? That is so dangerous! Can't you see I'm trying to make a meatloaf?"

The simplification process actually started with cable television, which streamlined our lives by giving us more than seventy channels for viewing. Cable was followed the personal computer, which simplified our lives beyond imagination—provided we regularly supply it with expensive maintenance and software programs, system upgrades, Internet connection, and additional memory.

Never content with a little simplicity, we further simplified our lives with the wonders of e-mail. E-mail allows us to correspond with people we used to visit in person, engage in leisurely conversation with over dinner, or even wave out the window and yell, "Hey, Martin! How's it goin'?"

Our lives have been so simplified by technology that I have but a fading memory of when we used to have personal contact with friends and neighbors. Strolling down the driveway to the mailbox and opening hand-written notes is now nothing more than a quaint remembrance.

Voice mail simplified our lives so that we never miss a phone message. After using the phone or returning home after a brief absence, I obediently check the dial tone (similar to Pavlov's dogs salivating upon hearing bells) for phone messages. If there is a pulsating tone, I hammer in a series of twenty-nine key-pad combinations that allow me to retrieve, delete, and save some 637 gazillion messages.

It is such a simple process on my new portable phone that I repeat it approximately eighty-nine times a day, consuming what some jaded souls claim to be the better portion of my waking hours.

Those jaded souls are the ones still using old-fashioned phones—the ones that force the user to walk the receiver back to the wall unit and hang it up, whereupon the user picks it up again the next time it rings. Not in this house. Thanks to the ease and simplicity of the portable phone, when our phone rings, we race through the house, bouncing off walls, sliding down hallways, and lunging at closed doors, straining to hear where the ringing may be coming from—in the kitchen, under a bed, or perhaps beneath a sofa cushion next to the long-lost remote control.

I'm not sure if you can ever take a good thing like simplicity too far, but I began to wonder when my Christmas list consisted of: a paper shredder, pager and home copier.

Nonetheless, we have continued to surge forward in our quest for simplicity. If a portable phone in the house is good, a cell phone we can take with us when we leave must be even better. With the sole intent of advancing our simple lifestyle—and the fact that my husband does his best shopping in electronics stores—my sweetie gave me a cell phone for Valentine's Day. The phone came with four brochures, one programming card, a warranty booklet, a quick-reference card, and a seventy-four-page instruction booklet. Being technology savvy, I immediately discarded them all. I knew exactly what to do. I turned the phone over to a teenager. Twenty seconds later, the kid showed me how the whole business worked.

I recently had the privilege of witnessing a woman elevate the free and simple way of living to a fine art form. She was in a strip mall parking lot struggling to lift a fifty-pound bag of dog food out of a shopping cart while she cradled a cell phone between her chin and shoulder and yakked away at 450 words per minute. Refusing to release the phone or pause her conversation, she showed remarkable dedication to the freedom we now enjoy through technology. Which is why I yelled at her, "You go, girl!"

She looked up, dropped her portable and her dog food, lost her footing, and stepped on her car keys, which set off her panic alarm (a marvelous electronic gadget designed to simplify automobile ownership). With her car's headlights flashing, horn honking, and a siren wailing, I just kept walking. A woman that dedicated to simplicity didn't need me complicating things.

Without question, the greatest beauty of modern technology is embodied in that cell phone. I offer as evidence the new national pastime of eavesdropping. It's not a hobby most of us have intentionally pursued. It's more like a slow-moving cold front or a bad hair day, something beyond control, foisted upon us against our will.

I was again engaged in this new pastime while standing in line at the post office. I had settled into wait position, prepared to study the collectors stamps in the glass display case, when the woman next to me whipped out her cell phone.

"Hi. It's me. I'm in line at the post office. He e-mailed me. Can you believe it? He e-mailed me!"

The commemorative stamps from the 1900s were intriguing: Crayola crayons, the teddy bear, the first World Series.

"He's out east. He wants to see me. Yeah? Can you believe it? What a jerk. The only way I'd see him is if he showed up with the money he owes me."

The 1920s commemorative stamps include flappers, radio entertainment, and a stamp with a woman casting a vote at the ballot box. Interesting stamps, but I still found it hard to tune out this resounding voice a mere twenty-four inches from my ear.

I had no intention of eavesdropping. I did not wake up and think to myself, "You know, you ought to bounce out of bed and see what juicy personal conversation you can tap into at the post office today." Yet, more and more, I find myself an unwilling participant in very public private lives.

I was meandering down the pop and chip aisle at the grocery when a nice-looking man passed by, headed the opposite direction. We smiled, nodded, and three steps later, I heard him ask, "So, what's your schedule look like this week?"

I was just about to say, "I'm flattered, but I'm married," when I saw that he was talking into a cell phone. That kind of occurrence is not only annoying, but it can be very hard on a middle-age woman's ego.

Two aisles over amid the rows of canned green beans was a woman on a cell phone loudly discussing a recent injury. Soon, not only was her phone buddy informed of the injury, but everyone from baking supplies to canned goods knew about it as well: a fall on the stairs, left knee.

Meanwhile, back at the post office: "I just told him, I'm in a new relationship and it's going great. It is going so great. The only thing is, my biological clock is ticking and his isn't. Hey, I'm not getting any younger. My clock is about to go off."

This woman was so intense she had given the impression that her biological clock could explode before the next customer filled out a return receipt request. Which is why, when the postal clerk yelled, "Next!" fifteen people broke from single-file line formation and stampeded forward in an effort to avoid further details on the frantic ticking of the biological clock.

Even Emily Post, remembered on one of the 1920s decade stamps, would back me up when I say that the post office, the grocery store, and the mall are not appropriate places to publicly discuss private matters via cell phone. Absolutely not. That kind of thing is best done in the privacy of one's car, during rush hour on the interstate. Or at a crowded four-way stop—while you're messaging the microwave oven to start a round of cordon bleu, which would be the perfect dish to set the mood for a ticking biological clock.

chapter

9

Reach Out and Ring Someone

Four cell phones in the family and we are now suffering the Curse of the Cell Phones. Many people consider cell phones a blessing, but those people aren't married to my husband, The Checker.

Checkers are people genetically predisposed to checking things like door locks, storm fronts on the Weather Channel, and departure and arrival times for all manners of travel. These are not—I repeat not—the type people you want freewheeling with three thousand free night and weekend minutes.

Brrrrring. "Hello," I say, knowing full well it is The Checker.

"I'm leaving work," he says. "I should be home before long."

"Good. See you soon." I hang up.

Ten minutes later, another brrrrring. The Checker strikes again. "I'm getting on the interstate."

"You called to tell me you're getting on the interstate?"

"Yes, and to let you know the northbound traffic is clear. What's new?"

"You can find out what's new when you get home. We can talk for free in the kitchen."

Ten minutes later, brrrrring. "It's me again," he says.

"Why does that not surprise me?" I ask. "Exactly where *are* you?"

"I'm at the south end of the subdivision. I just went over the speed bump and am approaching the stop sign. What are the kids doing tonight?"

"COME HOME AND FIND OUT!" Click.

It's enough to make you want to reach out and touch someone. But not in a nice way. This tool that was to bring safety and security to the family and increase vital communications and aid in times of emergency has turned into a weapon of harassment.

If you think my Checker is scary, consider this: There are millions out there just like him. We recently attended a get-together on his side of the family that included eight families, nineteen pagers, twenty-three laptops, and sixty-four cell phones.

Meet my sister-in-law, a Checkerette. Two of the fellows go for ice and she becomes concerned because they do not return according to her timetable. Even as a non-checker, I, too, am concerned—we desperately need ice.

The Checkerette grabs a cell phone. "Where are you two?" she asks. "Oh, yes, uh-huh. I see." They are in the parking lot about to walk in the door. Score another one for a Checker armed with a cell phone.

The party is barely over when five young adults and three cell phones commence the two-hour drive home because they have assorted work, school, and social commitments calling. In truth, they are worried Uncle Bob is going to get out the Scrabble board again.

One hour after they are gone we get a brrrrrrring. "There's trouble on the interstate. We've been sitting here for an hour. Thought you'd want to know before you and Dad start out."

Finally. The much-criticized cell phone has been vindicated by a third-generation Checker. It is indeed a worthwhile tool of technology. Fifteen minutes later, another brrrrrrrring. It's the youngest member of the wagon train, offspring of myself and my Checker. "Mom? Mom? Can you hear me?"

"Yes, sweetie! What is it?"

"I brought home my four-cheese manicotti from the restaurant last night and left it in Grandpa's refrigerator. Would you and Dad bring it with you?"

"Tell you what, sweetie. You head on home and we'll follow. When we get there, Dad will call you from the driveway and let you know if we remembered."

Talking It Over

Women don't go out to breakfast to eat. They go out to breakfast to talk. Talking is the female species' primary form of coping with stress. I've explained this a hundred times to my husband, but he still doesn't understand how I can go out to breakfast at six o' clock on a Saturday morning, come home after nine, and drop a piece of bread in the toaster.

"I thought you went out to breakfast," he says.

"I did," I answer.

"Well, what did you have to eat?"

"A scrambled egg and half an English muffin, but that was more than three hours ago."

"Why didn't you eat more?"

"Because I can't talk fast when my mouth's full."

"What in the world can you talk about for half the morning?"

He has now presented me with an awkward set of circumstances because, according to the International Rules of Breakfast, women don't divulge what they talk about. Cautiously, I attempt to explain:

"I am not at liberty to tell you precisely what we talked about because it is highly classified information, and if I were to tell you, I would then have to kill you. And that doesn't seem like a very pleasant way to start the weekend."

"Well you could at least give me a hint," he grumbles.

Oh, fine. I explain in the vaguest of generalities that this morning we covered kids, kids, kids, male attitudes, how to cut a template when wallpapering, the Euro, turquoise jewelry, and whether a Neon is wider than a Ford Escort. Oh yes, and skin types.

He gives me one of those you've-got-to-be-kidding looks and wryly asks, "Isn't it difficult to jump from home improvement to foreign finance?"

"Not at all," I say confidently. "The goal of breakfast is to cover as much ground as we possibly can in a limited chunk of time. We don't expect it all to fit together, which is why we were also able to touch on Schwan's peppered bacon, the providence of God, possible terrorist targets, school newspapers accepting advertisements, insurance deductibles, and the body count from Viagra. We also talked about Nu Shu."

"What's that?" he naively asks like a fish going for bait.

I explain that Nu Shu was a secret "women only" language that has been discovered in the hill villages of southern China. The language was developed over hundreds of years by uneducated peasant women assumed to be illiterate.

"What's more," I continue, "In imperial China, the penalty for creating new languages was death. Like that would scare off a woman who needed to talk. With Nu Shu, Hunan women could chat with one another in a language only they could understand. They could secretly communicate about the drudgery of domestic life by embroidering the flowing and feminine Nu Shu characters onto fabric or weaving them into cloth.

"Somewhere deep in the hills of southern China there probably is an ancient dish towel bearing the hidden hand-embroidered message: 'We wandered in the mountains for six hours yesterday, but could he admit he was lost?' Or perhaps one day someone will find a delicately woven shawl with a graceful geometric trim that is actually a series of Nu Shu characters meaning: 'If he reads aloud at the table one more time, I'm going to choke him with his own chopsticks.'

"The concept of a 'women only' language is not a novelty. By my calculations, at least four distinct dialects of 'women only' languages are alive and thriving in the United States today.

"Mother Tongue is the dialect most often spoken on the phone, as well as in groups of two to five in school parking lots or grocery store aisles. Using Mother Tongue, women hash over the antics and accomplishments of their children with a passion, angst, and animation that is foreign to most fathers. After a twenty-five-minute round of robust Mother Tongue, women find they are able to return to the duties of mothering with a lighter heart, a faint smile, and a renewed spark of hope.

"Girl Talk is the language women use to discuss the opposite sex. The purpose of Girl Talk is never to bash men or condemn men, but to simply reaffirm that, on the whole, men often behave as if they're nuts. By affirming our relational differences and analyzing the male mind, motiva-tion, and behavior, women are able to continue caring for the men in their lives in a tender and civilized manner.

"Sister Speak is the rapid-fire dialect women use when

discussing pregnancy, hormones, mammograms, and body changes. Sister Speak is a breezy give-and-take in which women compare notes on vitamins, allergy treatments, discount shoe stores, low phone rates, and reliable heating and air-conditioning companies.

"The most important dialect of all may be Psychobabble. This is not to be confused with the psychobabble of popular culture, television talk shows, or self-improvement books. No, this is Psychobabble as in women need to babble to keep from going psycho. When stress builds to the volcanic eruption level, the best release is to babble to another woman about hectic schedules, unreasonable time demands, and long days. The woman listening doesn't have to fix anything or solve anything, but simply appreciate the mental health value of one woman babbling to another."

Enduring my quick rundown on the four languages of women, my husband now looks dazed. I've seen this look before. It reminds me of the time I was out to breakfast with a couple of friends and a man we knew stopped by to say hello. That was his first bad move. His second bad move was saying yes when we asked if he'd like to sit down for a bit. After five minutes, he stood up, announced that our ricocheting from topic to topic made his head spin, and walked back to his table with three other men. At best, they probably covered two, maybe three subjects. Amateurs.

I continue my attempt to illuminate: "Women have always talked and will continue to talk two thousand words per minute, speak in sentence fragments, and switch topics in mid-paragraph because we are multi-tasking—chatting, thinking, eating, drinking, and listening all at the same time. We forego continuity and logic links in subject matter in favor of a steady stream of consciousness because we know this will be the last time today, perhaps in weeks, or even months, that we will have the freedom of saying whatever is running through our minds without having it over-analyzed, contradicted, dissected, or directly challenged."

My husband squints his eyes, tilts his head, and says, "That's crazy."

"No it's not," I say. "That's therapy."

11

To Know a Purse Is
to Know a Woman

My husband believes that I am the Imelda Marcos of handbags. He will tell you that I probably own somewhere in the neighborhood of 452 purses, one for each day of the year and four for every major holiday, including Arbor Day.

I actually own—well, it's not important how many purses I own. As a matter of fact, if you knew how many purses I owned, you'd probably feel sorry for me and say, "Lori, let's go shopping for purses."

Why does my husband believe I own a myriad of purses? I led him to believe it. A while back, we were in a department store and I stopped to look at purses on sale. "So, do you buy a purse every week?" he quipped. Sharp stuff coming from a guy who frequently asks if I have room in my purse for his car keys, Certs, telephoto camera lens, four-pack of film, paperback book on baseball stats, running shoes, and blade to the mower. You would think he never heard of the old cliché, "Never bite the handbag that totes you."

Being that he made a comment so clearly deserving of harassment, when we are ready to go somewhere, I now say things like, "I can't leave until I move things from my Wednesday purse to my Thursday purse." Or, "Should I carry my First Day of Fall purse, or my Groundhog Day purse?"

He suspects I'm joking, but he's not sure. He's always been an observant person; it's just that purses are not among the things he observes. But men should pay close attention to women's purses. You can learn a lot about a woman by the handbag she carries.

A female who carries one of those tiny purses no bigger than a slice of bread is packing nothing more than two lipsticks, an eyeliner pencil, her driver's license and a major credit card. This woman is either very young or very rich. She is also usually very thin.

I don't like her.

Women who carry mid-sized shoulder bags are light-years beyond needing only cosmetics and identification. They are packing coupon folders, bills to be mailed, and bundles of punch cards that say things like, "buy twelve loaves of bread and get a loaf free." This is the purse of a survivalist. This is a woman with children. She is also the designated pack horse for the entire family on everything from trips to the library to vacations to the Smokeys. Her purse warehouses sunblock, stamps for postcards, emergency manicure supplies, anti-bacterial hand gel, saltines wrapped in cellophane, and dried fruit snacks. This is the woman to approach in case of hunger or medical emergency.

A woman with an enormous purse resembling a backpack or bowling bag is one of two types. She is either a woman with a baby, consequently packing diapers, towelettes, teething gel, chubby books, strained carrots, and plastic play toys, or she is a grandmother who needs the extra space for all those eight-by-tens and five-by-sevens of the grandchildren.

To know a purse is to know a woman.

12

Sweet Scrubs

Our house may not look huge from the outside, but trust me, some days it is enormous. Granted, it's only a fraction of the size of these swanky new houses that look more like convention centers than homes, but nonetheless, our house is plenty big.

Despite our home's ample size, with two adults and three teens under the roof, there are days when we do feel a bit cramped and crowded. Someone mumbles about needing a basement. Someone else wonders how we have managed without a rec room, a pool table, and ping-pong table, while yet another party questions how much longer we can survive without one of those wall-size television screens and an in-home theater.

Someone else mentions that the family room is too small to accommodate a party for five hundred of her closest friends, while another voice suggests the possibility of knocking out a couple of walls and building on a small addition—say, something in the modest eight- to nine-thousand-square-foot range—and throwing in an in-ground pool and tennis court for good measure.

Some days, this entire family carries on like this house is so dinky that it's a marvel the city zoning commission gave us a street address. Why, the way these walls are closing in, we should all be on medication for claustrophobia. Come to think of it, it is probably just this side of a miracle that the five of us have been able to live in these tight, cramped quarters without elbowing one another on an hourly basis.

Yet the minute I mention cleaning the house, something strange and mysterious happens. The house, which only minutes ago was judged to be on the cramped and confining side, instantly mushrooms into an expansive villa twice the size of anything the Vanderbilts ever dreamed of owning.

Dust the furniture in every room? Ha! I might as well announce that we are going to wipe every speck of sand from the Sahara Desert. Vacuum? Was I serious? Surely not the entire house in one day.

This house, the very same one that sometimes cramps our style and provides minimal personal privacy, is now the size of the Roman Coliseum. Oh yes, did I want them to sweep that out as well?

Wash and wax the kitchen floor? Sure, and they'll be happy to hose down Buckingham Palace if I think that needs it, too. And, maybe the track at the Indianapolis Motor Speedway also could use a wax and polish.

It's not just the inside of the house that has a way of fluctuating in size; the lawn has a bizarre way of shrinking and expanding, as well.

When it's time to mow and trim, the yard swells from an average suburban lot to acreage suitable for raising a thousand head of free-range cattle. And when it's time to wash the windows, we might as well be talking the Empire State Building.

Take a little advice from a homeowner who lives in a

house that can go from crackerbox to estate in under sixty seconds: If you hear grumbling that your home is cramped and crowded, don't call a remodeling firm. Just set a vacuum cleaner and a sponge mop in the middle of the floor.

We normally split the cleaning chores for the estate on Saturday mornings and give the old mansion a quick shakedown, but there are days when I find it absolutely delightful to do the cleaning myself. Some days, when I'm working at home, I unexpectedly give myself the day off (far easier than giving myself a raise) for the express purpose of spit-polishing the house.

The first thing I do is scrub and wax the kitchen floor. I clean it the way my mother and grandmother always did. On my hands and knees. Odd, you say. You wouldn't say that if you could see the floor. The job may take the better part of an hour, but I thoroughly enjoy myself. The floor once again has that see-myself shine.

I know women aren't supposed to admit to enjoying such menial-type labor, but I sometimes do. And no, I'm not wearing heels, an apron, and a single strand of pearls. I am simply one of those oddballs who loves the smell of Pine-Sol and Murphy Oil Soap. I relish streak-free windows, the gleam of stainless steel, and Formby's Lemon Oil Treatment. All of this is probably strange enough to nab me a spot as a guest on the Jerry Springer show. The audience will hoot and howl and harass me as I describe the joys of cleaning cobwebs from the corner of the family room and flipping the cushions on the couch. I, in turn, will spritz them with a 3:1 vinegar and water solution and advise them on the proper techniques of using the Swiffer.

In any case, after finishing the kitchen floor, perverse as I am, I tackle the black hole of every kitchen: the cupboard that holds plastic bowls and lids. It used to be clothes hangers that brazenly reproduced during late night orgies. Today, the culprits are tubs and lids.

The promiscuous hanger problem abruptly ended when manufacturers began producing hangers made of plastic. Something happened. Hangers discovered chastity. Every plastic hanger I have ever purchased has been celibate. Oh, your cheap wire hangers will still wildly reproduce at the back of a bedroom closet in an occasional late-night orgy. But overall, hangers are now close to achieving zero population growth.

Plastic containers have taken up where wire hangers left off. A monogamous relationship for your average tub and lid is downright laughable. Sure, they pair off for a while, going through the routine of refrigerator, table, dishwasher, and drawer. They seem happy and then, the next thing you know, one of them switches partners. Lid swapping, tub swapping—I've seen it all.

Once the kitchen is in ship-shape order, I declare war on shower scum and blue blobs of toothpaste hardened on the bathroom sink. Wet towels are airlifted from the towel bars and floor to the washing machine. I fling open the window and the entire bathroom breathes a sigh of relief.

Bedrooms are dusted and tidied, and miscellaneous clutter is sorted between trash bags, dresser tops, and a box for Goodwill.

For the grand finale, I loop the entire house with my High Performance N2000 Carpet Cleaner and beat the living daylights out of four matted throw rugs. And while this, too, is a revolting confession, I must say I have a jolly good time.

This is a female thing. When you're pregnant and this

mood strikes, it is called nesting. When you're not pregnant and this mood strikes, it is known as domestic therapy, getting in touch with your inner homemaker. (For the record, I was stricken with the latter, not the former.)

It is about the pride and satisfaction that come from keeping house. It is more than the thrill of seeing two tons of junk mail disappear from a countertop. It is a feeling of victory and empowerment that comes from imposing order upon disorder, from drawing organization out of chaos. It is the joy found in making a house a home.

With the kitchen glistening, Mr. Clean nodding his shiny bald head in approval, and the Tidy Bowl man whistling a happy tune in his new dinghy, there is only one thing left to do—whip up a batch of chocolate chip cookies. By four o'clock the house smells delicious and I am shoveling cookies on a platter in anticipation of the troops blowing in after school.

It is doubtful the troops will notice my day's work, the disinfected bathrooms, or the sparkling floors. I'll be lucky if they notice *me* as they stampede to the cookies.

Bowlers find happiness in a two-hundred game. Pitchers revel in a no-hitter. Computer hackers exude a feeling of satisfaction when they have cracked the White House Web site. For me, pleasure is an entire house that is dusted, aired, vacuumed, and polished. I thoroughly enjoy it for the entire five minutes it stays that way.

13

Soiled Again

They say that gardening—digging with your hands in the rich, black dirt, tucking tiny, delicate seeds into the earth's breast, and watching them grow—is a wonderful way to relax. They lie.

I offer as proof an endless array of seductive books on weekend gardening. They lure, they tease, and they entice by claiming that with only a few hours on a Saturday, you can enjoy the rich rewards of a luscious and tranquil garden.

My favorites are the books written by a husband-and-wife team that talks about how they love cruising to the nursery on a Saturday morning, breathing the moist air of the greenhouse, picking up a flat of pansies, and ambling back home. They have a cozy arrangement where he digs the holes and she gently drops in the tender plants.

With the exception of the leisurely Saturday morning part, they sound like they might be regular people—until you read their credits. They start by thanking their mothers, their fathers, their grandmothers, and their great uncles who passed on their love of gardening and who, oh by the way, just happen to be third- and fourth-generation members of the Green Pea Society and founders of the Honorary Cultivators of Digitalis Purpurea. All of a sudden, they're talking gardening pedigrees and a foreign language that sounds like a handbook of infectious diseases.

My blood pressure was at least twenty points lower before I started trying to grow Oriental poppies. For five years I have tried, and for five years I have failed. Miserably. I tried leisurely starting them from plump seeds. I tried casually planting robust roots and eventually graduated to vibrant mature plants. I watered them, nurtured them, talked to them, and gave them the best mulch of my life.

For four years I got absolutely nothing in return for my efforts. Nada. Zip. Nunca. The closest I came to experiencing the reward of gardening was two years ago, when a poppy stem sprouted two inches before withering and falling over limp on the little plant marker that read, "Oriental Poppy: Roots quickly, matures into vividly colored, large-blooming plants. Easy to grow, thrives in any soil."

The way I see it, gardening promotes relaxation the way smoking promotes healthy lungs.

"Why not give up on poppies?" my family would ask as I returned from the nursery with yet another gorgeous, unsuspecting poppy specimen, my eyes glazed over. "Can't you find another hobby that relaxes you?"

"Give up? Thank goodness Churchill's family never talked to him that way," I answered.

"Why can't you just walk away?" they asked a week later as I polished my garden trowel and eyed yet another newly acquired perfect poppy.

"Walk away? Where would Microsoft be if Bill Gates just walked away?" I snipped.

"Why can't you be happy with marigolds?" they cried.

"I'd sooner grow goldenrod," I answered indignantly, taking in four deep cleansing breaths and tapping the third robust specimen in three weeks from a pot.

Maybe I'm too competitive to be a relaxed gardener. Twiddling my green thumbs tainted with root rot, I have often stood forlornly beside my phantom poppies, which should be a blaze of color, and gazed over my neighbor's fence. I have watched as his poppies flourish, grow taller, explode into bloom with flowers the size of satellite dishes, then lean my way to whisper in the wind, "Nyeh, nyeh, nyeh, nyeh, nyeh!"

A weekend gardener acquaintance mentioned that her tulip bed was looking gorgeous this year. Sensing a challenge, I said, "I put in a few new bulbs myself last fall."

"I put in nine hundred," she said with a gleam in her eye.

If you ever want to feel totally worthless about your backyard berry patch or the big pot of tomatoes sitting on your apartment balcony, surround yourself with professional weekend gardeners.

I was having dinner with some professional weekend gardeners when one of them asked if I had a garden. That question might as well have been a wheelbarrow loaded with fresh compost coming at me full-speed, but I didn't see it. "Sure I do," I said. "We've got tomatoes, peppers, and raspberries."

"Do you can a lot?" one of them asked.

"What's to can?" I said. "Most days we eat what we've grown before we get it to the kitchen sink."

I'm certain I detected a look of sympathy.

"Do you freeze much?" another asked.

"Bagels, pizza, and waffles on a weekly basis," I answered.

"Oh," one of them said with a hint of disbelief. "Carol over there put up twenty-five quarts of tomatoes, twenty jars of strawberry jam, ten quarts of pole beans, and fifteen pints of sweet corn. Course, that's just from her little quarter-acre garden." Carol sat up straight and gave a slight nod in recognition of the attention. I had the distinct impression the other women thought that if Carol would spade up another few square feet and really put her mind to it, she could use her time and talents a lot more prudently.

To me, a relaxing garden is a modest patch of black soil you can pace off in a few leisurely strides and neglect six days out of seven. To professional weekend gardeners, a nice-size garden is something that takes a half-hour to tour on the back of a John Deere lawn tractor. Their gardens have signs that say, "Big Boy Tomatoes, Turn Left," and "Pole Beans, Next Exit."

I water my puny little patch with a squirt from the garden hose while professional weekend gardeners chatter excitedly about underground irrigation. When they laugh and boast that their gardens could easily supply the city of Chicago with three daily servings of leafy greens, I join in the boasting and claim that my garden could easily feed a family of five (rabbits). When they talk of their chives and oregano being robust, I add that my basil and parsley are exceptionally fine. (They were a dollar off a jar with an in-store coupon.) When they moan and groan about hoeing and weeding, I, too, drop my head and agree that the thistles are particularly bad this year (which is why I never touch them).

Professional weekend gardeners are fond of saying things like "playing in the garden" or "just drop it in, turn your back, and watch it grow." Their most sadistic little pleasure, though, is dropping by to check on your shriveled little weed patch and asking if you can use a few tomatoes. They just happen to have six bushels they can't use just sitting in the car.

Professional weekend gardeners can extol the therapeutic values of gardening all they want, but I'll just say this: I never knew relaxing could be so exhausting.

Pictures, Anyone?

There are two kinds of people: those who take pictures of vacations, birthdays, and family events and get them developed, and those who take pictures of vacations, birthdays, and family events and let them rot in the camera.

My brother's family is the latter. They take pictures; they just never develop them. Well, at least they don't develop them until they are sure the film has been expired for several years.

Their routine is to shoot a half-roll of film and let it sit in the camera until the next major holiday/wedding/graduation/reunion. Nine months later, they finish off the roll, pull it out of the camera, and throw it in a kitchen drawer, where it incubates for another year. One day, when my sister-in-law is rooting around for birthday candles, she finds the roll of film and tosses it in her purse. Six months later, she's standing in line at the pharmacy and digging for a breath mint in her purse when she sees the film and decides to get it developed.

They are not alone. I have a friend who has her daughter's kindergarten, eighth grade, and high school graduation pictures all in the same shoe box.

"What are you waiting for?" I ask.

"The wedding," she answers. "I want to get all the pictures in one album."

My brother just picked up a roll of twenty-four exposures he recently had developed. There were pictures of their house, their car, their boys, and their dog. They sold the house seven years ago. They unloaded the car when cassette tape players were hot. The boys, he didn't recognize. His own have changed so much he's not sure it was them. Maybe they were the kids from down the block. The dog in the pictures went to that great big fire hydrant in the sky many moons ago.

My husband is from the school that believes film should be processed immediately; sooner if there's a coupon in the paper. He treats family pictures like he's working on deadline for CNN Headline News. Pictures are processed, chronologically ordered, and notated for time, place, weather conditions, and the price of gasoline per gallon.

My husband recently whipped out nine packets of film from our summer vacation to show to the extended family. My brother is not the type who will yawn or excuse himself to the bathroom to avoid looking at other people's pictures. No, he will look you dead in the eye and say, "Why would I want to look at your pictures? I don't want to look at my own." Then he will yawn.

We know he's kidding. At least my husband thinks he is. I announce that I feel a bout of malaria coming on and retreat to the opposite corner of the room to wait and see what will explode.

My husband proceeds to methodically unload nine packets of color prints. He announces that the pictures will be passed counter-clockwise, placing the picture you have just viewed at the back of the stack to keep them in order. There are 324 pictures documenting every inch of our 2,800 mile jaunt up and down the East Coast. Passing of the pictures will be followed by a multiple-choice and true/false history and geography quiz.

My brother looks across the room at me and scowls.

I yell, "Smile!" and snap a quick one.

If he's nice, maybe I'll get double prints and give him a copy in seven years.

chapter

15

Gullible's Travels

You should try to time your family vacations to coincide with natural disasters. We have had the good fortune of doing this for a number of years now, and I must say, it is very relaxing. By way of clarification, let me point out that we don't *cause* the natural disasters: We simply follow them.

One of the best examples of this unnatural knack for natural disaster was the summer we chose to make our first-ever visit to that famous Florida theme park, the host of which is a mouse on steroids and his girlfriend, Minnie. We planned the trip in the middle of January—long before the lightning strikes that sparked extensive forest fires in the bone-dry Sunshine State. Apparently scared off by the recent fires, a number of travelers changed their plans. Not us. We weren't about to lose our pricey deposit on the hotel room.

The longest wait in line for any of the immensely popular thrill rides that give you whiplash and a stiff neck was only fifty minutes. Huge stretches of Florida's I-95 smelled like we had just missed the state's biggest jamboree campfire. Sure, our clothes and luggage all reeked of smoke, the car still has that up-the-chimney smell, and our travel was somewhat slowed by all the emergency vehicles, but what the hey. At one rest stop, although the toilets were closed and every last vending machine was locked up, the kids were able to visit with real live, extremely smokey, and utterly exhausted National Guardsmen who had been hauling out burnt timber. Now tell me a travel agent could arrange that for you.

In the third year of our marriage, my husband and I arranged time off from our jobs to take our first real vacation, a scenic visit to Mount Rainier. Two weeks before our departure, nearby Mount St. Helens blew her top. Clouds of volcanic ash traveled clear past Idaho. Mount Rainier, like Mount St. Helens, was also a dormant volcano, so naturally the entire world immediately canceled reservations to any and all destinations west of Pittsburgh.

My husband and I found the lodge at Mount Rainier to be charming as well as enormous. Large spaces are like that when you have them all to yourself. With the exception of two hikers and one bear, the park trails were virtually deserted. The hikers had been out of touch with civilization for weeks. They'd been wondering what that loud boom was. And the bear never had been real keen on newspapers or electronic media.

We missed the peak of Midwest floods a few years ago by just a few hours. We routinely pass that way at some point each summer to visit my side of the family. Even in the event of a flood, it's not the kind of trip where a cancellation would be entirely understood. Some of the exit ramps to the factory outlet malls were closed, and a number of the fast-food joints had been encircled with sandbags, but interstate traffic really zooms when flood waters are lapping at the shoulder of the road. We never made better time.

Tornadoes? Been there, done that—six years ago in the peaceful Amish countryside of northern Indiana. We drove right into the heart of a menacing storm. We sat it out by the side of the road and watched Dorothy, Toto, and the ruby red slippers all whirl by only inches from our noses. We thought it might well be our last natural disaster vacation. But the storm passed and we continued our trip home past splintered trees, twisted silos, and barns hammered into the ground. The kids were never better behaved or quieter. Actually, it was early August before the fright wore off and they resumed normal speech patterns.

Global warming? Been there, done that, too. One of our first family vacations with the kids was spent touring the St. Louis riverfront. With the exception of blistering heat, it had been an uneventful trip. No rain, no hail, no electrical storms, earthquakes, blizzards, tornadoes, or meteor showers. Just heat. Lots and lots of sweltering heat. One of the girls began complaining that she was hot.

I grabbed her pudgy little hand and snapped, "We're all hot. I'm hot, your dad's hot, your brother's hot, your sister's hot. Do you hear us complaining that we're hot? No. That's because when our family goes on vacation, we expect to get hot. We expect all kinds of terrible things to happen when we go on vacation. Now quit complaining and happy up."

The next day she broke out with chicken pox all over her little body.

Two years ago we went to a family reunion at a state park in the scenic pine hills that border the western edge of Nebraska. Picturesque setting. Decent cabins. Each and every one filled with large moths the locals fondly referred to as millers.

The millers only came out at night. They dropped through the ceiling tiles; they weaseled their way in through window screens and door casings. The more playful ones would jump out from behind the shower curtain or hide deep in the toaster or the coffee maker. The millers came by the hundreds, and in some cases, by the thousands. We fought them with brooms, fly swatters, rolled up newspapers and even tried filling a dish pan with lots of suds and holding it to the light, which the locals said would cause the millers to dive into the water and drown themselves.

The millers were so huge you could hear their wings flapping after turning out the lights and burying your head beneath the covers. After two nights, we gave up trying to eradicate them. We started naming them. We even trained two of them to light the outdoor barbecue.

So the accommodations weren't four star. We survived. Sure, the youngest still sleeps with her head beneath a blanket every night, but it's only been two years. She'll come around.

Weary of thrill vacations with insect infestations, tornadoes, forest fires, and volcanic eruptions, we thought a vacation to our nation's capital with museums sheltered from the elements in temperature-controlled environments would be safe, predictable, and entirely uneventful.

Wouldn't you know, we timed our trip to D.C. to coincide with the biggest natural disaster to hit our nation's capitol in years—Bill Clinton and Monica Lewinsky.

16

The Jury Is Out

Of all the requests the average person receives for a chunk of his or her time, my guess would be that the little envelope that delivers the notification for jury duty elicits one of the most negative responses. Personally, I wouldn't mind being called for jury duty if just once I were actually seated on a jury.

With my most recent jury summons, it looked as though I would finally do something besides sit and wait. After one hour of waiting, the bailiff calls a string of names and collects questionnaires—including mine. Excitement builds. The bailiff disappears.

One hour later he returns and leads us through three sets of complicated instructions. Wait here. Wait there. Come wait here again. There's nothing like waiting to raise a body's stress quotient.

His fourth directive is a variation on a theme: Go wait by the elevator. But first, anyone with weapons, knives, or mace should relinquish them before passing through the metal detector on the way to court. Prospective jurors glance nervously about.

I glance nervously about, then slowly slink forward holding my two-inch red pocket knife with one small blade, a file, tiny scissors, a plastic toothpick, and, most important, tweezers. For the record, my pocket knife has never been used in any sort of terrorist attack. Three years ago, I thought about using it to cut a window in the dark and claustrophobic jury pool room, but I have never once used it for bodily harm, other than plucking eyebrows.

After being herded onto elevators and directed to the fifth floor, we are instructed to wait some more. More waiting; more stress. After waiting and waiting and waiting, the bailiff instructs us to group together as we might be moving into a real, live courtroom sometime before noon. Skeptical, but compliant, stray potential jurors congregated on the east side of the hall quietly shuffle to the west side of the hall.

A woman wearing a red dress and black pumps mentions that she needs to use the ladies' room, which is just around the corner. She asks if I will let her know if any action breaks loose. We both laugh at the prospect of anything happening and she disappears. I wonder if this is it, the peak of my civic duty to man and country, to be a liaison between the women's restroom and the court system. The woman in red has been gone fifteen seconds—just long enough to round the corner, swing open the restroom door, choose a stall, and set her purse down—when the bailiff materializes and announces, "Courtroom C—let's go! NOW!"

Finally, we enter a real courtroom and fourteen members of our group are called to the jurors' box. It is clear the objective of those in the box is to find a way out. I, however, would permanently sign over my little red knife (including the tweezers), my earrings, and my shoes to be in the box. I would even give up my bottle of Tylenol to do something—

to do anything—as opposed to sitting and doing nothing.

The prosecutor asks if anyone in the box watches *Law & Order*. A few hands twitter. *Ally McBeal?* Two hands twitter. I would gladly volunteer that I watch *Matlock*, but the prosecutor doesn't care what I watch because I'm not in the box.

Now the prosecutor wants to know if prospective jurors can tell the difference between attorneys and detectives in court, and attorneys and detectives on television. Prospective jurors want to know if the prosecutor is simple.

The defense attorney asks a woman about her first impression of the defendant. Her impression is that he is a nicely dressed man. My impression is that this is the first time he's had a shirt and tie on in years and that he is slouching and looking out of the corner of his eye because he knows in a few minutes it's all about to hit the fan.

When asked if anyone in the jurors' box has a reason he or she cannot serve, hands do not hesitate nearly as much as they did on the *Ally McBeal* question. One woman takes medication that makes her drowsy; a bald man wearing suspenders and dangling a toothpick from the corner of his mouth isn't sure he can be fair; another man has good tickets to a playoff game.

Another hour has passed when five jurors are dismissed. Sitting, waiting, stressing, I eagerly listen as more names are called. I could be fair. I could be alert. I could even wear suspenders and chew on a toothpick if that's what it takes to get on a jury and do something tangible.

The second group shuffles forward, and a smattering of people are left behind. Fate has again determined that my civic duty is to be one of the hundreds of stiffs who do nothing but sit and wait.

It's just as well they took my pocket knife. The longer I sit and wait, the bushier the bailiff's eyebrows look.

17

Mom on *COPS*

Earlier this week, I stopped at a red light, looked both ways, then made a right turn. There was a big black and white sign that said "No Turn on Red." I didn't notice the big sign. I probably never would have noticed it, except that someone else did. A policeman.

As I was turning right on red through the No Turn on Red intersection, I caught the eye of a police officer in cross traffic. I didn't catch his eye exactly. I caught his arm and finger wildly pointing at the sign and pointing at me.

I slapped myself on the head, mouthed, "I'm sorry, I'm sorry," and continued on my way. Slowly. Very slowly. As I watched the officer in my rearview mirror make a U-turn, I considered the possibility that he might be interested in further discussion. I was right.

His flashing lights went on and I pulled to the side, heart racing, palms sweating, lump in throat.

One of my earliest memories of kindergarten is learning that the police officer is our friend. Despite the 1968 Democratic National Convention, the Rodney King incident, and a few blips on the radar screen, I still believe that to be mostly true. So I didn't know why I was scared to death. I take that back. I knew exactly why I was scared to death. I sometimes watch the television program *COPS*. All right, so now you know.

Not only am I a lawbreaker, I also watch *COPS*.

The officer comes to the car and I am so panicked, recalling a Seattle episode where a crazy woman was yanked from her car and thrown to the ground, that I frantically push the up button instead of the down button on the automatic window.

With the window finally down, I apologize profusely and admit that I am completely in the wrong. He takes my license and registration and returns to his squad car. I return to my memories of previous *COPS* episodes.

My nose is running. That happens when I get upset. There is a box of tissues in the back seat, but if I reach for it, he could think I am going for a gun and I could be history. I saw a guy go for something in his back seat on a New York *COPS* episode. It was a sawed-off shotgun, not a decorator box of Puffs, but the point is they blew out his windows and nailed him in seconds. I decide that tissues are out of the question.

My window is still down and I am freezing. If I roll up the window, he could think I'm hiding something behind the tinted glass. I saw a guy roll up a window on a Miami episode of *COPS* (he was hiding drugs) and before you could say, "Call my attorney," they were frisking him spread-eagle on the hood of his car. I decide that freezing feels good.

Besides, without the window down, how else could I study the faces of fifteen billion passing motorists with smug looks that say, "Loser!" and "Way to go, moron!"

These are the same drivers hitting their brakes, slowing down at least twenty miles per hour, and suddenly driving with their hands at ten and two. *And* they are all using turn signals.

The officer returns to my car, where I sit with running nose and chattering teeth. I flinch. It's sheer reflex. The officer is nice and professional and gives me a ticket with a huge fine. I assure him that I have learned my lesson.

I also have learned I should probably stop watching *COPS*.

18

Policy No.
389#%&57%^@39204

One of the surest ways to receive a generous dose of
stress is to get involved with a managed health care
program.

Several months ago, our family doctor bailed out of our
managed health care program, or the "network" as they
say down at the 1-800 number. To make things even more
fun, the obstetrician I've seen for years left for a medical
missions trip to Africa. All things considered, it's just as
well. They were both hopelessly old-fashioned.

They were so out-of-date that, when you called either of
their offices, a real person answered the phone. This was
terrible for their professional images, but these physicians
were as stubborn as their stethoscopes were cold.

Now we find ourselves in a quandary. Do we go with a
doctor in our managed health care booklet whose phone is
answered by an automated voice-mail system? "Press one if
you're naive enough to think you can get an appointment
within the next forty-eight hours; press two if you think
you're having a heart attack and would like instructions on
how to administer your own CPR; press three if you'd like

to listen to an instrumental rendition of Barry Manilow's hit song 'Mandy.' Please stay on the line. Your injury and illness are important to us."

Or maybe we should go with the doctor whose phone message simply says, "If you'd like to make an appointment, visit our Web site at www.thephysicianisyourfriend.com."

I certainly don't want to get anyone in trouble with the health insurance industry, but our former family doc was so antiquated that he once personally called our house on a Saturday to see if my husband was responding to medication. It was enough to make us wonder if the man would take a whole chicken and quart of canned peaches in lieu of a fee.

What's more, both of our former doctors would often chitchat for an entire minute or two in the examining room before whipping out a tongue depressor or ordering x-rays. For maximum profit, many managed care programs prefer that doctors keep patients moving at a brisk rate of twelve per hour, or about five minutes per visit. It takes me twice that long to fight my way into a paper gown, but who am I to question progress?

The OB/GYN, in particular, was notorious for asking patients about their general health, then taking a seat and actually listening. Patiently. Once a year, I would recite a list of complaints ranging from weight gain and energy loss to the pull of gravity and frequent mood swings, and then ask if he thought I was crazy.

Each year, he would carefully review my chart, bob his head a couple of times, and then say, "When we talk about crazy, we're talking about an extremely wide continuum. I think you still have a long way to go."

Working from a list of approved doctors, I am now searching for one still in the network, reasonably close to where we live, and willing to become "primary care physician" to five more patients. About once every fifteen minutes, I strike paydirt and get a real person to talk to and find a doctor whose practice isn't full. I then call the health care management office to have this doctor designated as our primary care physician. The health care representative then says, "Will you hold while I check my computer screen for the status of that doctor?"

I say, "Yes," and proceed to look about the room for laundry to fold or start cleaning the drip tray beneath the stove burners, or some such project that will give meaning and purpose to my life as I whittle away hours on hold.

The agent returns to the line and tells me there seems to be a problem. "Could you hold while I check a second computer screen?"

"Yes."

She puts me on hold again, and after a lengthy delay, which gives me time to empty the dishwasher and mop the entire kitchen floor, comes back to tell me the last four doctors I have inquired about are "no longer in the network." Four times I inquire about a new primary care physician; four times I am told they are no longer in the system.

She thinks I don't know why she puts me on hold each time, but I do. It's so she can laugh her head off and tell Susan, in the cubicle next to her, that she's got a live one on line three. It's also so she can have an opportunity to go to yet a third computer screen and play another round of Solitaire, which is in my best interest really, lest I get the mistaken impression that managed health care was designed to provide prompt and personal service.

As of four o'clock this afternoon, I have scribbled down

so many network I.D. numbers, phone numbers, and Web site addresses in my search for a primary care physician that I'm not sure whether I have been pre-certified to shampoo my own hair or if I now possess the computer code to the nation's missile defense system.

On the upside, I have resisted the urge to beg one of our 1-800-Whatever-The-Last-Person-You-Spoke-To-Told-You-Is-Wrong health care reps to come to the house and break both of my arms—an event that would be infinitely more fun than playing Dialing for Doctors (although not covered by group policy No. 389#%&57%^@39204).

The most important thing I have learned from maneuvering my way through managed health care is this: The road to crazy isn't nearly as long as the OB/GYN thought it was.

19

Hold, Please

The phone rings at 7:35 A.M. I can hear my mother on the other end, but she can't hear me.

"Hello?" Mom says.

"Hello!" I return.

"Hello? Hello?" she shouts.

"Hellll-oooooo!" I holler in response.

Nothing.

I can hear Mom telling Dad that she can't hear me, so I hang up.

The phone rings again at 7:39.

"Hello?" Mom says.

"Hello!" I answer.

Once again, I can hear Mom, but she can't hear me. This time I can hear something else. It is a commotion in the background. It is my Dad and nephew telling Mom she must be doing something wrong with the phone. They're leveling incompetency accusations at Mom. Mom is vehemently protesting in self-defense, and a level-two fracas is well underway.

The three of them are in my nephew's hospital room,

trying to call and give me an update on his condition. For some reason, I can hear them, but they can't hear me.

I hang up the phone and call the hospital. I ask them to ring my nephew's room. The pleasant switchboard operator says she is sorry but can't ring rooms before eight o'clock. I tell her that my mother has tried to call twice, and I am sure that everyone in the room, if not the entire floor, is alert and awake.

I ask again if she wouldn't please try? No, she won't try, but she will transfer me to the nurses' station and I can ask them to try.

"Would you hold, please?" the operator asks.

"Sure," I answer.

Music music music music music music music Music music music music music music Music music music music music music music Music music music music music music music music music music music music music music music music music Music music music music music music music music music music . . . *Are you one of the five million with undiagnosed diabetes? Although some people show symptoms of thirst, weight loss, and fatigue, others show no symptoms. That's why a diabetes test is so important. Ask to talk to a diabetes educator for more information* . . . *Music music music music music music music music Music music Music music music music music music.*

The voice giving the diabetes warning is warm and friendly. He'd ring a patient's room before eight o'clock. The voice wasn't one of those metal, robot computer voices, but the voice of a real man. He sounded sincere, like he has the disease himself or has someone in his family who does. I begin feeling a little thirsty. And tired. Maybe it's that new pillow I've been sleeping on. Then again, the pillow isn't that new. But I don't think I feel 100 percent. As a matter of fact, I don't know when I've felt so thirsty and tired at the same time.

Music music music music music music Music music music music music music music music music music music music Music music music music music music music music Music music music music music music music Music music music music music music music music music music Music music.

"Nurses' station," a voice answers.

"Yes, good morning," I respond. "My mother has been trying to call me. She's with my nephew in room 320, but when they try to call out, the connection isn't any good. The switchboard operator said that perhaps you could ring his room."

"Sorry, we can't ring into the rooms from here, but I can give you back to the switchboard."

Before I can say "dirty syringe," she has put me back on hold.

Music music music music music music music music music music music music music music music music music music music music Music music music music music music music music music music music music music music music music music music music Music music music music music music music music music Music music music music music music music music music music music music music music music music music music

. . . Did you know that even mildly elevated blood pressure can injure your kidneys? Did you know that even slight

elevations pose a double risk of kidney failure? If you suffer from hypertension, talk to your doctor . . . *Music music music music music music music music music music music music music music music music. Music music music music music music music music music music music music music music music.*

There's that man's voice again. He speaks with such authority that I am just sure he is a doctor. Or George Clooney.

Boy, am I thirsty. Parched is more like it. And tired. Even worse, my head has a dull throbbing action going on. Yes, I think I feel the onset of a headache. I being to wonder if this is a hypertension-related blood pressure headache. I also feel a catch in my side. I'm not sure what it is, but I am positive it's coming from the vicinity of my right kidney.

Music music music music music music music music music music music music music music music music music music music music Music music music music music music music music music music music music music music music music Music music music music . . . *Shortness of breath can occur with exercise, but if it occurs excessively in times of rest or inactivity, it may be a symptom of heart disease. If you're experiencing this problem, see your health care provider* . . . *Music music music music music music music music music music music music music music music music music Music music music.*

I am so thirsty. If I was on the portable phone, I could at least get to the sink. Oh well. The headache seems to be subsiding. The pain in the right kidney is better, too. Well, not better really, just relocated. It's now coming from my left kidney. Actually, the kidney pain and headache are nothing compared to this shortness of breath.

Music music Music music.

"Switchboard," the operator answers.

"Hi, I talked to the nurses' station and they can't ring into the rooms," I say.

"Well, didn't you tell them to walk down to the room and tell your mother to call you? I'll ring the nurses' station and stay on the line with you this time."

Before I can say, "Calling out doesn't work! I need to call in!" she has me on hold.

Music music Music Music Music music music music music music music music music music music music music music music music music music music music . . . Did you know that most hip fractures result from falls? Hazards are right outside your home. Slippery, wet walkways may be unavoidable, but you can reduce most hazards inside the home. Use guard rails. Move obstacles like furniture and electrical cords. Use non-slip pads under rugs. Ask our fitness experts about exercises that may improve balance . . .

Music music Music music music music music music music music music music music Music music music music music music music music music music music music music.

I'm thirsty, I'm tired, I have a cramp, and now my breathing is shallow. If I can just stretch the phone cord, I think I can reach that orange juice on the counter. WHOA, BABY!! What IDIOT left a science book in the middle of the kitchen floor?! It's a miracle I didn't break a hip! You wouldn't think your own kitchen would need hazard cones and flares!

*Music music music music music music music music music music music music music music music music music music music music Music music. *

I compose myself and try for the orange juice again. Stretching, stretching, stretching. The cord won't reach. The orange juice is just inches out of reach. I am absolutely wasted and it's not even eight o'clock. The inside of my mouth feels like a cotton ball, I have shortness of breath, early stages of kidney failure, and I'm sprouting a bruise the size of Florida on my right hip. Who would believe that a half hour ago I was set to do Tae Bo for beginners, the twenty-minute workout?

I'm trying to stay calm, but I must ask how hard is it for a hospital that can rip open chest cavities and do entire heart transplants to RING A SIMPLE PHONE IN A SIMPLE ROOM?

*Music music music music music music music music music music music music music music music music music music music music Music music. *

"Nurses' station."

"Yes," says the switchboard operator, "She's trying to reach room 320. Could you go in there and tell them to call her? I'll put you on hold while a nurse goes to the room."

"Wait! WAIT!" I scream, my heart racing, my head pounding, my tongue sticking to the roof of my mouth. "The problem is they can't hear me when they call out—"

Music music music music music . . . . . . Did you know that stress can be hazardous to your health? To handle pressure, practice relaxation techniques. Try meditation every few hours. Exercise regularly. Slow down and have lunch or a friendly chat with coworkers. For more information on stress management techniques, talk to your health care provider.

chapter

20

Taking Care of You

On the stress scale, this isn't a big one, but it still makes me wonder: When did the people who hand you a restaurant menu, take your order, and bring food to your table become caretakers? I just love it when a server arrives at the table, crouches down at eye level, and says, "Hi, I'm Brandon and I'll be taking care of you today." This is the most dangerous trend in dining since the return of the high-fat Caesar salad.

Chances are Brandon is twenty-two, has one ear double-pierced, and has the tips of his hair highlighted orange. When Brandon says he'll be taking care of me today, he has no idea that he is playing with fire. Brandon is clueless that he's talking to a woman who has been taking care of others for the past twenty years—and quite naturally gets very excited when someone announces they are going to take care of her.

My initial response to Brandon's pronouncement is "Great! Draw me a hot bath, put fresh sheets on my bed, lay out a clean nightie, and then hit the road." Obviously, I don't say that because it would be entirely inappropriate.

Nor do I say, "Wouldn't you like to know *my* name? How long do you think this arrangement will last? And by the way, I have a crook in my right shoulder, would you mind?"

It's not right that these servers, er, caretakers, keep getting my hopes up. When I've been shopping and running errands and a server announces he's going to be taking care of me, it takes a lot of self-control not to say, "So, you think the brown sweater is all wrong, too, don't you? Take it back and get a credit on my charge card. Oh, and the canned goods go in the cupboard next to the sink, and just leave the trash bags, laundry soap, and dish soap on the shelves in the garage."

But no, I don't say any of that. Speaking so candidly would scare a kid like Brandon clear out of the food service industry. Who knows, it might even scare his hair back to its natural color. Instead I just bite my tongue and say, "Can I get the dijon vinaigrette dressing on the side?"

A second, yet equally disturbing, trend in dining is the use of that ever popular phrase "you guys."

I walk into a restaurant with female friends and the host or hostess says, "How are *you guys* today? Would *you guys* like a table or a booth? Can I get *you guys* something to drink?" The *you guys* phenomenon is even more puzzling than the announcement that a total stranger is going to be taking care of me today.

I look around the table and survey my female friends, henceforth known as "the guys." None of us guys has facial hair. At least not anything noticeable in dim light. None of us guys is now nor ever has been a Sumo wrestler. All of us guys are wearing mascara, blush, lipstick, and undergarments that support curves guys do not have. Hey,

I don't want to make this an anatomy lesson. No, this is a vocabulary lesson.

I am not a guy, nor am I one of the guys. Please do not call me a guy. If all the servers out there are really serious about wanting to take care of me, that's probably a good place to start.

21

Memory Bank(ruptcy)

K nowing that short-term memory loss is often a symptom of stress, I was fascinated to learn of a chess master who played three twelve-year-old opponents in simultaneous games. To even the odds, the chess champ also played blind-folded.

One question comes to mind when I hear about a guy with a memory like that: Has that man ever found himself standing in his garage saying, "Now, what did I come out here for?"

Probably not. He probably never came within inches of leaving one of his kids in the restroom at the Eisenhower Memorial in Abilene, Kansas, either. And he probably never mailed a crystal bowl to a cousin for a wedding gift, forgot about it, and sent a check two weeks later. But does that really make him a better person than me?

The vast majority of us are far more likely to find our-selves standing in the garage talking to ourselves than playing chess blindfolded. So why is it that we view forgetfulness like some grave character flaw and consider a good memory a cardinal virtue?

Memory is overrated. How reliable is a brain function that won't let you remember where you left your car keys twenty minutes ago? How user-friendly is a mechanism that allows you to recall six of the seven items you need at the grocery, but withholds the green onions until the instant you pull in your driveway?

At least women have plausible justification for forgetting a few things now and then. We've spent the best cells of our memories recalling details for other people. Our brains are loaded with important facts and figures, like inseam sizes and sleeve lengths, cholesterol levels, who likes creamy peanut butter and who likes crunchy, car pool rotations, furnace filter measurements, and due dates on video rentals. Women around the globe would be simultaneously playing six games of chess, boiling pasta, and balancing checkbooks while blindfolded if we weren't constantly besieged by family members who are themselves hopelessly memory-impaired.

Nevertheless, it is time to give forgetfulness some well-deserved recognition. Although quiet, shy, and not nearly as flamboyant as memory, forgetfulness actually has some very positive qualities.

For starters, forgetfulness is good for business. If everyone had perfect recall, it would wipe out massive segments of the economy devoted to memory enhancement. Film and camera companies like Kodak, Nikon, and Sony could forget about their financial futures. And don't think the phone companies wouldn't miss those forgetful folks who are always making just one more quick long-distance call because they suddenly remembered something they forgot to say a half-hour ago.

Forgetfulness is also good for relationships. It's uncanny

how many marital arguments draw to a close when one party finally forgets why he or she was mad in the first place. Only by forgetting how your kid went nose-to-nose with you an hour ago can you can hug the daylights out of her now and mean it with all your heart. The slow, but eventual, ability to forget is a healing salve.

Fear, pain, and suffering elbow their way into our memory banks and make themselves comfortably at home. They would forever needle us with their sharp and piercing jabs, were it not for forgetfulness gently softening their brittle edges.

The key to being at peace with your memory is admitting that you can't remember everything—and that some things are better left forgotten.

22

Web Site
Technology

Getting a Web site is like getting a puppy. Looks cute, looks fun, looks like it would enrich your life. Two weeks after you bring the critter home, you realize this is a lot more puddling, yapping, and scratching at the door than you bargained for.

My son, who helped get my site up and out of the doghouse, thought it would be a good idea to teach me some basics so that I could start maintaining www.loriborgman.com myself. I had agreed to a training session before I found out that his idea of teaching was to have me stand behind him while he moved at lightning speed through six software programs, 409 computer screens, and a flurry of keyboard commands. He then spun around and said, "Did you get it, or do you need me to go over it again?"

"I got the part where you opened up the icon that said 'My Computer.' Everything after that was a blur," I said.

Totally exasperated, he turned back to the computer, again whipping through software applications, computer screens, and keyboard commands. But this time he also flew off his chair and BAM! zapped a small button on the stereo.

"What does that do?" I asked. "Change the background color? Change the type?"

"It changes the radio station," he said, with a look of disbelief.

"Why did you do that?"

"Because I can't work when there's a commercial on."

There it was, the missing link to effective Web design, handed to me on a silver platter—commercial-free FM radio.

Finally, I was allowed to sit in the computer chair myself.

My instructor began barking orders, "Save it as a JPEG. Now change screens. Minimize that screen. Close that window." I took commands, whipped that little mouse around, fought off carpal tunnel symptoms, zipped from screen to screen, and hammered in commands when BAM! I hit the stereo and zapped it to the oldies station.

BAM! My instructor zapped it back to alternative rock with a warning that you absolutely cannot update a Web site listening to "Splish, splash, I was takin' a bath."

"C'mon," I said. "All my friends listen to the oldies when they work on their computers."

"And if all your friends jumped off a cliff, would you want to do that, too?" he fumed.

Maybe it was my imagination, but my son had the same look on his face that Mr. Silverman, the junior high counselor who also taught industrial arts, had on his face when I broke my wooden letter holder in half in the vice. It was during the two weeks of the school year when the girls took shop and the boys took home economics with Miss Grove, a pretty brunette and the first person in our school to wear contact lenses. Home ec was old hat, but shop was completely foreign to me. The tools were new. Measuring was new. Sawing was new. Hammering was new. Mr. Silverman's face was not new. In the course of the first week, twice Mr. Silverman had had his face only inches from mine. But then, twice in the first week I had snapped my letter holder in half in the vice. After the second accident, Mr. Silverman got real close to the my face, turned beet red, and very slowly said, "Take your seat and don't get up. I'll make a letter holder for you."

Mr. Silverman was like my son—nice but a stickler for detail. I heard he took early retirement the following year.

In any case, my son was giving me a Mr. Silverman look. Then his face softened, he took a deep breath, and the next thing I knew he told me I was ready to update a page on my own. He rattled off a few hundred instructions on how to make a link and told me to get started. "And this time," he asked, "can you work on your speed?"

I began working and he began "teaching" some more: "Mom! An index has to be html, not just htm! I already told you that once."

Duh! How could I have forgotten?

I hadn't had this much fun since my husband and I wallpapered the bathroom with vertical stripes.

I continued working. He continued teaching.

"Make it a link!" he commanded. "A link! Can you figure out which menu icon would mean a link? Think World Wide Web! Which picture is like a world? Look for the one that is round and green and blue."

Sarcasm is so unbecoming. And I'll tell him. But not now.

"Look, Mom," he said, "this is taking a lot longer than I planned. I've got some plans and some things I'd like to do."

"Fine," I said, "don't let me keep you. You've been a big

help. Really. And don't worry about the Web site. So it will look like hackers have vandalized it. I'll live. You go on with your friends and have a good time. I'll be just fine."

"Listen," he says, "If you're not done by 11:30, call me. I'll be on the cell phone. I'm going to a movie now. Afterward, we're going to get a bite to eat. Do you want me to stop back after the movie?"

"No, don't worry about me. I'll be okay. But do be sure to keep the cell phone on just in case there's an emergency—like I delete your hard drive or accidently find your personal e-mails."

Just like that the kid decided to stay home. Teens. They're so fickle.

I continued working. He continued teaching and monitoring and breathing down my neck and looking over my shoulder.

My question was this: If I was now working on my own, why could I feel the kid's hot breath on my neck and his eyes boring holes in the back of my skull?

I remember a time when I stood behind him oozing frustration and exasperation as he sat on a piano bench, fat little fingers unable to do a simple task like find middle C or tell the treble clef from the bass. I also remember rolling up *The John Thompson Easy Piano for Beginners* book and fighting the urge to whack him over the head.

Here we were with the tables turned. Well, not quite. This Web page computer manual is three inches thick. There's not an outside chance he could roll it up and use it. I'm positive. I've been watching him try for the past three hours.

chapter

23

Change

In answer to the concerns of my family that I do not adapt well to change, I would like to say—balderdash. Why, just this morning I came up with a plan that will allow me to never again worry about keeping pace with change. My ingenious plan revolves around three magic words: living history museum.

As you know, these are popular tourist attractions featuring buildings and artifacts from the past, where people in heavy costumes sweat bullets and give guided tours rambling on about what life was like in another age. Given the current speed of change, I have every reason to believe that such a person could be me, in my own home, sometime in the next few years. Or twenty-four hours.

It will be a tour especially designed for young people and will begin like this:

"Welcome to our home. As you step in and we get started, may I point out that the period costume I am wearing today consists of khaki pants with a buttondown shirt tucked neatly inside the waistband. Both pieces are all-cotton, machine washable, and require light ironing."

"You actually own an iron?" a girl asks, giggling behind her hand.

"Yes. It was one of the last ones Wal-Mart sold before the world went perma-wrinkle."

"What's that wrapped around your middle?" a young man asks.

"This?" I ask, pointing to the leather band threaded through loops on my pants. "Why, this is a belt. For centuries belts were used to help hold pants in place and keep them from sagging."

"Wow," a kid says. "So you don't sag?"

"No," I answer. "Well, at least my pants don't."

"Now if you would turn your attention this way, I'd like to direct you to the kitchen. For generations, this room was the hub of a woman's existence. We relied heavily on appliances such as stoves and refrigerators."

"But-but-but," stammers a puzzled blonde looking at the refrigerator, "where's the icemaker?"

"No icemaker," I explain, shaking my head. "A long time ago people made their own ice cubes by filling trays of water and placing them in the refrigerator's freezer. During family holidays, running out of ice was a welcome excuse adults would use to flee the house and disappear for hours at a time under the pretense of picking up a few bags of ice."

"But if there's no icemaker, then there's no water dispenser on your refrigerator. How did you drink?"

"Excellent question, sweetheart. We would take a glass from the cupboard, walk over to the tap, and get water from the sink. The sink is where we also did dishes."

"By hand?" a kid asks, with a look of astonishment.

"Yes, it always worked better than using our feet. Now, as I open the refrigerator door you can see that it is filled with carrots, celery, broccoli, mushrooms, cantaloupe, and honeydew."

"What's wrong with them?" asks a young lady with a gasp. "They look—they look—enormous!"

"Ah, yes. You see, once upon a time, fruits and vegetables did not come pre-washed, pre-cut, and pre-packaged in clear plastic, disposable clam shell containers. Homemakers used knives and cutting boards to prepare their own foods for cooking or baking. These foods would then be served to the family over there."

"Where?" asks a kid, peering out from beneath his ball cap. "On that weird pool table without pockets?"

"Exactly. Only it's not a pool table. It's a dining table. Before the drive-through, carry-out McMeal became the standard, we used to set the table with dishes and silver-ware. The family would gather around to share a meal and exchange tidbits about what happened during the day."

"I heard my mom talk about that once," says a young man wistfully. "It's called dinner or something, isn't it?"

"Yes. You really are a fine history student. From here we go to the family room. Over in the corner you will see—"

"Wait, wait," a young man interrupts. "May I? I think I know this one. It looks like some sort of a workstation where you store financial records, pay bills, and keep important documents. In concept, it's something like a laptop that threw up volumes of paper."

"Bravo, young man. You have just identified a roll-top desk!"

"Yes, but what's *that*?"

"This?" I say, holding up a box of floral stationary and a fountain pen. "Why these were once the staples of per-sonal communication. You would write personal letters, thinking-of-you notes, or thank-you cards to friends and family."

"Sort of like e-mail with a built-in graphics card?" the youth asks.

"Exactly!" I say.

"So you used stationary, like I send animated greeting cards over the Web?" He then scratches his head and says, "But without a 750 megahurtz computer, modem, and cable hook-up, how would it get there?"

"By mail," I answer. "Cards and letters could be dropped off in a mailbox. The post office, a monolithic inefficient government bureaucracy, would sometimes, despite every effort to the contrary, deliver letters and cards to the correct address anywhere in the country."

"What was the monthly hook-up fee?" a young girl asks.

"No hook up fee, dear, merely a stamp. See this one. It's an old one. If you want to see something fascinating, watch this. You tear the stamp out of the little booklet and lick it."

"Ooooooooooh," the crowd croons in unison.

"Yes, this is dodally wedwo," says the young lady with the stamp stuck to her tongue.

"Pardon?" I say.

"This is totally retro," she says, placing the stamp on an envelope as the glow of Christmas morning sweeps across her face.

"And right next to the stamps is a Day-Timer. Each box represents a day of the week. This is where we mark down activities, appointments, and important phone numbers we need to remember."

"PALM PILOT!" the chorus screams together.

"Yes! Now on the coffee table you will see a variety of newspapers, magazines, almanacs, and the *New York Times* best-selling books."

"How long did it take you to download those and print them out?" a tall brunette male asks.

"We didn't download them. We bought the periodicals and books at bookstores and the newspapers were delivered to our home."

"You're saying you didn't get any of this online? You went outside your house and paid cash for these things?"

"You've got it," I say.

The wheels are turning in a short kid with a bad cowlick as he muses, "So this was sometime after the fall of Rome, but before the Intel chip and e-commerce?"

"Aren't you a quick study?" I say, giving the kid a pat on the back.

"Now does anyone know what this is?" I ask.

"My parents used to have one," said a freckled red-head. "The black disk that looks like a flattened frisbee is played under an arm contraption with a needle. The disc rotates and the needle sends sound waves through those two huge rectangles that are speakers. The little boxy opening on the front is for a cassette tape. It's an MP3 that's not portable and has severely limited music choices. What's it called again?"

"A stereo system," I say.

"Now we come to what I believe is the highlight of the tour. Here it is, sleeping in this La-Z-Boy recliner. Does anyone know what this is?"

"On-site tech support staff member that collapsed?" guesses a lanky girl.

"No, try again."

"A FedEx man who got sore feet breaking in new shoes?"

"No, no, no," I say. "This is my husband."

"You mean your significant other?" shouts a kid in the back.

"No."

"You mean he's your life partner?" asks another.

"No, he's my husband. This is the man I married—"

"What number is he?" says a portly kid in the middle of the herd. "Second? Third? Fourth?"

"No, this is my first husband. We have been husband and wife for twenty-three years."

"Impossible!" says a wide-eyed boy.

"That's what my mother said, too, but you are both wrong," I answer with a smile.

"I didn't think people stayed married anymore," says the wide-eyed kid.

"Well, very often they don't. And sometimes it does seem that we are a little unusual."

"A *little*?" exclaims a kid with braces and a pierced tongue. "Are you on the historic register?"

"No, silly. But *Ripley's Believe It or Not* e-mailed us and would like to hear from us if we make it to the thirty-year-mark."

"What does a husband do?" asks a little girl.

"Basically, the role of the husband is to stay married to the wife."

"What does a wife do?" she asks.

"Stays married to the husband."

"Do they like each other?" she questions.

"Most of the time, but certainly not always," I say.

"What's in the husband's hand?"

"A remote control."

"Do all husbands come with those?"

"Yes, dear. It's standard packaging."

Heads shake and a murmur sweeps over the room. They thought living history might be mildly interesting. They were surprised it was downright fascinating.

"We're just about out of time," I say. "I do ask that you keep your voices down so you don't wake the husband. I believe we have time for one more question."

"I have a question," says a pretty olive-skinned girl in the front. "Did the husband and chair come together?"

"No, sweetie. In the beginning they all come separately. After twenty years, they are a matched set."

part 2:

You Always Stress the
Ones You Love

24

Mouth in Motion

When I consider the parts of my body that cause me the greatest amount of stress, first place goes to my mouth. It's an even tossup whether the things I do say or the things I don't say get me in more hot water.

I am cleaning the kitchen after dinner, thinking how fortunate I am to be married to a man who has never suffered a serious allergy to work. I am thinking how much I appreciate that his hard work has helped us acquire luxuries like a stove with a self-cleaning oven, a refrigerator with a self-defrosting freezer, and an automatic washer and dryer, none of which have required a major repair in at least forty-eight hours. Yes, I am thinking to myself with a wet dish towel in hand, life is good.

I am thinking how nice it is that my husband comes straight home from work instead of stopping at bars featuring exotic table dancers with names like Lacey Dreams and Cinnamon Spice. (I know about these things—I read the little ads in the sports section of the newspaper.) I am thinking how grateful I am that even when things haven't gone so well for him at the office, he doesn't snap at me, yell at the kids, or kick the dog. We don't have a dog, but if we did, I know he wouldn't kick it. Then the garage door goes up, interrupting my train of thought. He walks in the house and I snap, "It's after eight o'clock—why are you so late?"

We are riding in the car when my husband turns on the radio for the news. He listens to the news at the top and bottom of the hour even if the news hasn't changed for three days. It is one of his annoying quirks. We come out pretty even in the quirk department. I think how fortunate I am to have found someone who is able to tolerate my bevy of quirks (and no, I don't care to list them).

Yes, life is good. Life is very good, I think to myself, readjusting my seat belt and gazing at the barns and farmland passing by in waves of red and green.

I think about the comfort and security found in companionship. I am thinking about the way a couple grows closer with the passing of time, when my husband takes the exit ramp at seventy miles per hour, almost landing on the bumper of the guy ahead of us. "What are you trying to do, kill us?" I shriek. "A little closer and we could have had the pickle off the sandwich that guy's eating."

Back in the kitchen, pots and pans and cupboard doors begin banging. It is my oldest daughter, baking. She makes killer cinnamon rolls and always cleans up the half pound of excess flour on the floor when she's finished. I think to myself how delightful it is to watch her work in the kitchen. What a pleasure to observe how organized and methodical she is about tasks of any size. I pass by her and say, "Sweetie, I hope you greased the pan or you'll have to pry them out with a crow bar."

My son is in the garage, charging at a piece of wood with a power tool. Who knows what it is this week— rabbit trap, bow, hat rack. I am thinking what a good kid he is. No juvenile record, no school suspensions, no Dennis Rodman tatoos or metal sculptures dangling from a pierced bottom lip. I am thinking how enjoyable it is to have a kid who is creative and resourceful. I say, "Better not hurt yourself; I think we're out of Band-Aids."

My youngest daughter is gabbing on the phone. She is lying on the floor and walking her feet up and down the door frame while she jabbers away. I think of how quickly she is growing and maturing into a young lady with pleasant manners, a big heart, and a quick wit. She grabs a boom box, inserts a CD, and proceeds to blast it over the phone. "Hey!" I bark, "if you don't have anything to say, hang up the phone."

She hangs up the receiver, walks overs four inches from my face, and says, "Sometimes you act like we're all a giant pain."

Now how in the world could anyone say something like that?

I love my family. I think nice thoughts about them all the time. And not just when they're at school or at work. And not just when they're asleep. Many times I think nice things when we're right in the same room together.

Okay, so maybe I'm guilty. Maybe I think nice things more often than I say them. And maybe I am a little too diligent about saying negative things as soon as they pop into my head. It's the old Mouth In Motion Dilemma: I say the things I don't want to say and don't say the things I do want to say.

I remember to ask about homework, but forget to

thank someone for bringing in the mail. I remember to remind someone to put their laundry away, but forget to say thanks for starting that last load of jeans. I razz someone for not picking wet towels off the bathroom floor, but neglect to say thanks for calling when she was going to be late coming home last night. I drop a comment about a certain someone snoring like a foghorn that could rattle ships from the Atlantic to the Black Sea, but am remiss to thank him for staying up three hours to work on taxes after I went to bed.

Somewhere I read that it takes five compliments to compensate for every criticism. For every, "That paper looks like you wrote it with a pen between your toes," I directed at a child, I'd need counter balance with three "good hair day, honey," and two "way to match your shoes!"

Not long after reading that it takes five compliments to balance every criticism, I read that it takes at least ten compliments to compensate for every criticism. Then I read a Q&A by a psychologist who said that it takes fifteen compliments to compensate for every criticism. Shortly after that, I began avoiding any and all articles about how many compliments it takes to counteract a criticism.

Negativity is a habit like biting your nails or cracking your knuckles. What I need to do is reverse the habit: speak more of the positive thoughts and keep some of the negative ones to myself. This is what counselors call inhibiting oneself. They say inhibition can cause stress, but I think there are many cases where inhibition, in the words of Martha Stewart, "is a good thing."

My sixteen-year-old recently said that she thought mothers were a lot like meteorologists.

"How's that?" I asked, puzzled.

"You listen to what a meteorologist has to say to find out what the weather will be like," she said.

She paused, sized me up, and hesitated briefly before continuing, "And you listen to what a mother is saying to see what the family's day will be like."

"So what's your forecast?" I asked.

"Well, when you were unloading the dishwasher and tossing laundry baskets around, I would have said cloudy with a chance of tornado. But now that you've settled down, I'd say partly sunny."

"Thanks. I'll take that as a compliment."

Fourteen more years and she'll level out that thinly veiled criticism.

25

Just Because We're Married Doesn't Mean We're Compatible

Tradition has long held that the three greatest sources of stress in a marriage are sex, money, and in-laws. I would like to add a fourth—those cheesy compatibility quizzes in women's magazines.

They're so goofy, I don't know why magazines publish them. What's worse, I don't know why I take them. Believe me, I've tried to stop, but I can't. I see a quiz that says "Is It Love or Lust?" or "Is Your Marriage for Better or Worse?" and I'm sharpening the point on a No. 2 pencil before you can say "trial separation." I race through the questions, scanning the differences between a., b., and c., while flipping to the answer key in order to stack my points so that the better half and I emerge in the category of "eternal ecstasy," as opposed to "seek professional help immediately."

The quizzes are supposed to promote intimacy and understanding, but in our case, they invariably stir up unrest and discontent. I know this every time one of these doozies beckons to me, but I can't seem to help myself. ("Hi, my name is Lori and I'm addicted to relationship quizzes.")

The scenario predictably unfolds something like this:

I am reading a piece on fifty ways to speed up my metabolism when I happen across a page with an article titled, "The Six Steps to Sizzle." It is a quiz guaranteed to reignite the flames of romance in any marriage.

I look at the better half and myself and wonder whether this article has been written for us. Mr. Romance is unconscious on the couch, the remote control firmly in his grip, "watching" a ball game. He is breathing through his mouth, doing that little snort thing every six inhales or so. I'm sitting on the end of the sofa, eating a small bowl of vanilla fudge swirl ice cream (I emphasize the word "small"), being very careful not to scrape the spoon on the bowl so that a certain someone will not awake and remind me of a certain diet I put the two of us on last week. I am wearing no makeup and have on a pair of khaki pants and T-shirt I've worn for three days straight. When you work at home, you can get by with that sort of thing. Not a pretty picture.

I unilaterally determine that our marriage relationship is in need. In need, nothing. According to this article, Casanova and I are teetering (or sitting and lying in this case) at the brink of disaster. We may not be fighting, or at one another's throat, but that is not the point. The point is, we don't pack picnic baskets and steal one another away for lunch or sip champagne under the moonlight on the patio, which, according to the magazine, is a sure sign that our relationship is marking time on death row.

I resolve to rekindle the relationship. We will become new people, dreamy-eyed, star-crossed romantic saps who send special occasion cards for no special occasion. "The Six Steps to Sizzle" says I need to take a personal inventory of my beloved because, even though we are married, have three kids, and share a bottle of mouthwash, I can't possibly know him. The article says to begin by finding out his favorite actor, color, song, and food.

I nudge Don Juan and ask, "Who is your favorite actor?"

He opens one eye, looks at me suspiciously, and says, "Jim Carrey."

"Be serious, who's your favorite actor?" I repeat, deftly sliding my empty bowl and spoon behind a sofa pillow.

"Tell me this isn't another one of those marriage quizzes," he sighs.

"I'm just getting to know you," I say.

"We've been married two decades; what don't you know?"

"Your favorite color," I snap.

"Black," he growls, returning his eyelids to closed position.

"What's your favorite food?" I snarl.

"Everything you made me quit eating two weeks ago!"

"Your favorite song?" I bark.

"In-A-Gadda-Da-Vida."

Great. I strive to bring greater intimacy to the relationship and all he gives me to work with is Jim Carey, fried foods, and '70s rock.

"Every time you read those articles and put us through one of those tests, you end up in a snit," he mumbles.

"But we need to get to know each other," I counter.

"We do know each other," he says, getting up off the sofa.

"Where are you going?" I demand to know.

"To the kitchen for ice cream. You want some more?"

26

Wanderer

Marriage has a mysterious way of taking qualities you found absolutely charming in your mate when you were dating and turning them into grating irritations once you are bound until death do you part.

Before we were married, I thought my husband's slow, meandering, time-has-no-meaning quality was quite adorable. Two decades later, it drives me up a wall.

He so freely meanders that he is frequently hard to find. The stress in our marriage could be cut in half if some electronics firm would invent a small tracking device I could attach to him. The tracking device wouldn't necessarily have to give him a jolt when he wanders away, but rather give me, the tracker, a few hints and clues about the general direction in which my wanderer is headed. I'm thinking of something along the lines of those gizmos Marlin Perkins used to follow wildebeests across the African grasslands.

You know the type of wanderers I'm talking about. They are the people who say to meet them at the west gate of the ballpark, then twenty frantic minutes later you find them talking to an old friend in the concession line. Wanderers are the folks who can look you straight in the eye and say they'll be in the "vicinity" or the "area," when what they really mean is "somewhere this side of the Equator."

Let's face it. Some people simply don't have the herd instinct. As kids, they were the ones who resisted holding hands and walking in pairs. They never shed a tear when they were separated from their second-grade class on a field trip to the art museum. Wanderers are the people who instinctively take each and every meandering path that angles off the main road.

Five of us were hiking around a lake recently when my wanderer, also known for carrying a camera and taking his time to shoot scenes of interest, disappeared. I should have seen it coming. It started with a little lingering, followed by some blatant straggling. After a seemingly sincere, "I'll catch up in a minute," he was out of sight—abducted by little black helicopters for all I knew. I figured our best bet was to locate a park ranger and file a missing person report: male, brown hair, brown eyes. Wearing jeans and a blue jacket. Last seen circling the lake. About forty-eight years of age.

I have successfully remained married to a wanderer because I was raised by a wanderer. My mother is a high-speed wanderer you never want to let out of radar range in a shopping mall. She loses you around a coffee-maker display and it's like a small plane disappearing over the Bermuda Triangle. You might as well find a bench, put your feet up, and have a pizza delivered.

Sometimes at the grocery store, it helps to slow her down by loading her cart down with twenty-pound bags of potatoes, onions, and apples. But even that is no guarantee.

If she loses you, the best strategy is to sprint the entire length of the store, back and forth, checking each aisle. She may be temporarily hidden in some obscure crevice reading a product label, but eventually every wanderer must cross a main aisle to get to one of those less-traveled aisles.

What really gets me about wanderers is that none of them can admit that they are the ones who wandered away. Invariably, when they are found, the first words out of their mouths are, "Where have you been?"

My wandering mother likes to tell a tender little tale about a wife yearning for her deceased husband. The woman found comfort every night by looking into the sky, recalling her husband's promise to wait for her two steps behind the moon. One day, Mom told Dad that was such a nice idea that maybe they should agree to meet three steps behind the moon. "What's the point," he said, "you're never where you say you'll be."

True. But if he had a little tracking device . . .

chapter

27

Man Years

The mysterious huffing noises started several months ago. At first I thought it was a bouquet of wilting helium balloons deflating in bursts. Then I thought it was the storm door to the garage, making that gentle whooshing sound as it came to a final close.

The strange huffing and sighing noises increased in frequency. Gradually, they grew louder. It was almost as if they were in the same room with me. Puzzled, I searched high and low, inspected every room in the house, and checked the seals on all the windows. Finally, I pinpointed the source: my husband.

"So it's *you* making those noises," I said.

"What noises?" he asked.

"Those huffing sounds, like a bull before it begins to paw the ground and charge at the bullfighter."

"I'm not making any huffing noises," he insisted.

Thirty seconds later, he let out a long huff as he folded the sports section of the newspaper and opened the business section.

"There it was again," I said. "You huffed."

"I was simply breathing," he answered.

"Well either you have congestion or a serious respiratory problem, because that is not normal breathing; it is huffing and heaving and heavy sighing."

He got up from the table, let out a sigh as he knelt down to get the toaster out of the cupboard, then did a slow moan as he stood back up.

The sounds increased in frequency. He often sighed when he sat down on the couch and, more often than not, groaned when he stood up. One night he let out a deep sigh of exhaustion like he'd just completed ten laps around the track. He had moved five dinner plates to the kitchen table.

Soon after, he was walking out to the mailbox when a deep alpha-male groan rattled the entire house. My best guess was that, for some strange reason, he was bench pressing the piano. Actually, the electric bill had fallen to the floor and he had just picked it up. In all fairness, the envelope did bear the weight of one first-class stamp.

Later that afternoon, I heard a vintage Tarzan yell come from the garage. "Are you hurt?" I screamed, running in his direction.

"I was just hoisting the middle seat back into the minivan."

"Look," I said, "this has got to stop. The Big Bad Wolf didn't breathe this hard when he blew down the Three Little Pigs' houses."

"Hey, you make sounds, too, you know," he said.

"I do not," I snapped.

"Yes, you do. Every morning when you go downstairs I hear your knees click like crickets."

"Well they're just fine after a shot of WD-40, and anyway, that's entirely different. I can't control the sounds my knees make. But you can stop all this huffing and puffing and moaning like some old man on his last leg."

"I am old," he said.

"We're practically the same age, and you don't hear me huffing and moaning every time I move. Besides, how can you be old? You're only three years older than I am."

"Maybe so," he said, "but they're man years."

"They're *what*?" I asked, dumbfounded.

"Man years. You know, like dog years. Man years are harder on a body than woman years. Why do you think women outlive men?"

I couldn't believe what I was hearing. I slumped down into the nearest chair.

The sigh I let out registered a 5.3 on the Richter scale.

28

The Pear & I

One of the greatest sources of stress in our marriage has come from our disagreements about accumulating stuff. This is the natural outcome of a pack rat, or collector, as they prefer to call themselves, pairing with a minimalist.

My husband comes from a family that saves empty mayonnaise jars, old lawn mowers, and prescription pill bottles—because you never know when you'll need them. I come from a family whose motto is, "If you don't use it, lose it."

My husband thinks walls covered with pictures and shelves lined with knick-knacks is ideal. I think if the Amish did away with a few of the extras, they'd have a good handle on interior decorating.

If something is stationary, my spouse automatically considers saving it. Books, magazines, newspapers, school programs, greeting cards, ticket stubs. He seems to have a particular fondness for anything made of paper.

If I see something stationary, I immediately consider

discarding it. I toss magazines and recycle books as soon as I've turned the last page. I zing the rubber bands binding the stalks of broccoli directly into the garbage and never even wince when I throw away shopping bags.

You would think I would have recognized this polarization between us before we were married. Courtship blurred my vision.

Before we were married, we both moved from the tundra section of the Midwest to Oregon. My rented U-Haul accommodated my seasonally-organized and cross-catalogued goods quite nicely. His U-Haul was stuffed to overflowing, forcing him to choose between his bed springs and stacks of old newspapers. As a journalist, I followed his reasoning and even seconded the decision that left his bed springs curbside and bundles of papers loaded for the journey west.

I was in denial. Fully aware, I now regard his accusation that "Heave, Ho!" is my motto for living as thinly disguised organization-envy. True, I can't remember my car's license plate number, yet I have memorized the phone number to call to schedule a Salvation Army pickup. But that doesn't make me a radical—it's asking strangers for their Zip Codes and announcing what day of the month pickups are in their neighborhoods that make me extreme.

I am always perplexed by the pictures in decorating magazines (which I look at only in the checkout line at the grocery, because the last thing I want to do is buy one and add to the stash at home). There will be a family room with a gorgeous sofa, a matching love seat, and a contrasting wing-back chair. It all looks nice enough, but something is wrong. Terribly wrong. There's no stuff. No clutter. No unopened mail. No old newspapers piled anywhere. No mounds of things waiting to find permanent homes.

Let's start with the coffee table. The coffee tables in these magazines are always bare, except for a pear and two books on Tuscany. Do you know anyone in real life who has ever sat a lone, green pear on a coffee table?

I gave it a whirl to see what would happen.

The kids walked in the room, stopped dead in their tracks, and cautiously began circling the coffee table like it was radioactive.

"What is it, Mom?"

"What's it look like?"

"A statement on world hunger?" one offered.

"No," I said, "it's a pear."

"Yeah, but why is there only one and why is it on the coffee table?"

"I'm decorating."

"Really, Mom, if this is what that new diet is doing to you, it's just not worth it."

The lone pear on the coffee table was downright unnatural. Natural for us is a coffee table layered with books, videos, CDs, remote controls, magazines, and newspapers. Natural for us occasionally includes a few shoes and socks strewn about the floor. These decorator magazines would never show something that true to life. They don't even show television sets in their pictures.

Of course, that's only logical. These people are too upscale to watch television. They sit around and watch pears.

The kitchens are even worse. Check out the refrigerators. They're stark naked. Not a single school paper hangs from a cheap magnet.

I once attended a baby shower where an extremely bubbly hostess forced us to go around in a circle and answer the following question: If your house was on fire and your family was safe, what one item would you choose to rescue?

Nineteen out of twenty women said the refrigerator door. The refrigerator door holds a family's entire life— party invitations, magnetic letters, photographs, homework, artwork, wedding announcements, coupons, receipts, and rebates. A cluttered refrigerator door is to a growing family as a wet nose is to a healthy dog.

I also am enthralled with the pictures of kitchens that show bare countertops except for a gorgeous pedestal cake plate holding artichokes. This was no doubt the brainchild of the same person enamored by the lone pear. Sitting on my kitchen counter is a large pile of mutant tomatoes, the largest of which looks remarkably like Lyle Lovett. Next to Lyle sit a purple lunch box, the newspaper, two water bottles, a portable radio, and a roll of duct tape.

The area by the telephone in these photographs is laughable, too—not a dog-eared phone book or school directory in sight. Where, may I inquire, are the scraps of paper, junk mail envelopes, and beverage napkins with messages scrawled on them? Where in the world are they hiding all the stuff?

It's certainly not in the closets. The insides of these closets are obscene. They have nothing in them but clothes! Obviously, these are not real people living in these homes. It's been years since our closet looked like a closet. Each passing day it looks more like a miniature store'n lock. So many treasures, so little space.

The answer to our problem may be feng shui. Feng shui, touted as an ancient Chinese art (although it has all the markings of southern California), is the arranging of furniture and living spaces in such a manner that it allows you to be at one with your energies. For example, say you had a lot of money you didn't know what to do with. You would call a feng shui practitioner and he or she would come to your home, move your bed to the east, drape your bath towels at a different angle in the bathroom, relocate a large armoire smack in the middle in your front entry hall, and charge you $1,500 for releasing your personal energy.

Feng shui practitioners are now doing closets. For do-it-yourself types, they advise a simple three-step process.

Step No. 1: Clean everything out of your closets.

It would take me less time to raise a herd of cattle, butcher the meat, and wrap it for the freezer than to clear everything out of our closets. Feng shui practitioners insist that moving everything out of the closets will allow you to get at them with a vacuum and soap and water and (drum roll, please) release stuck energy.

I had no idea energy was stuck in the closets. Old 33-RPM albums? Bowling balls? Board games? Christmas decorations and ice skates? Yes. Trapped energy? No way.

We have so much stuff jammed in our closets that we could be talking a release of thermonuclear energy. But when I consider the stress that would be unleashed between my husband and myself, debating over what is worth keeping and what should be pitched, there is no point in even reading on to Steps No. 2 and 3 in the art of closet feng shui. The marriage means more to me than organized closets with free energy.

29

Shopping Stress

A lot of women say shopping relaxes them. Unfortunately, I'm not one of them. Case in point: If I had known buying a shirt at the mall for my husband's birthday was going to mean stripping half a man completely naked, I would have settled for the mail-order shoe shine kit.

I am cruising through a department store while suffering a severe case of shopper's block when—Bingo!—I spot the perfect gift for hubby. Sharp looking dress shirt with a complementary tie—20 percent off. I will be in and out of here in five minutes. It is a kamikaze shopper's dream come true.

Ten minutes later, I have pawed through forty-five shirts on the display table, each and every one of them a size sixteen or seventeen. Not a single size 15½ in the heap.

I look around for a clerk. Talk about a vanishing species. There is not another living soul within a six-department range. It's a wonder thugs aren't wheeling entire racks of Regis neckties out the door and into paneled vans in the parking lot.

While I don't seek a clerk, I do spy one more shirt. On a

mannequin. It is not a full mannequin, but a fraction of a mannequin. This mannequin has a chest, a rib cage, and a neck, but no arms or lower torso. A hunk of wood resembling a plunger doubles for his head. This is all the rage with mannequins today, to have them look like anything except real people.

There are mannequins with ghostly white skin looking as if they survived a terrible nuclear accident. There are mannequins with pinched faces that look like they've been shoved through a sausage stuffer, and mannequins with heads but no faces. There are female mannequins with detailed, anatomically correct chests, but with no hint of a rear end or a single fat deposit on either thigh. And they call that realism.

In any case, I am positive this half-a-man mannequin is wearing a size 15½ shirt. I would peek inside the back of the shirt to check the size on the tag, but the mannequin is perched on a shelf a foot above my head. I hoist the half-a-man down from the shelf and have my arms wrapped around him in slow dance position when an older couple walks by and glares. I shift the half-a-man to my side in more of a tango position.

The couple snorts and stomps away.

Unable to hold the half-a-man and simultaneously reach down his neck, I drop him to the floor and struggle to pull pins from his back to free the shirt. Obviously, the straight pins have been fired into the mannequin with a pneumatic nail gun. I find I am able to get more leverage against the straight pins if I lay the half-a-man flat on his chest—and put my knee directly between his shoulder blades.

Granted, this looks a lot more like a WWE SmackDown than shopping, but there is a principle at stake here: Never pay full retail. In the words of that great American shopper Patrick Henry, "Give me 20 percent off or give me death."

As I am thrashing about with the half-a-man, two women ask for directions to the restroom. A teenage girl wants to know where the Clinique counter is, and an older gent picks my purse off the floor and asks where he can find one in a dark brown. I figure I've got sixty seconds before store security shows up. And there are women who claim this is relaxing?

Two more tugs and I liberate the shirt. Size 15½. I knew it was.

Drained and exhausted, I drag myself toward the distant sound of a chiming cash register. "Did you have any trouble finding what you needed today?" the smiling clerk asks.

"No, I'm pretty well set," I say, smoothing my hair and putting my jacket back on. "But there's a half-a-man on a shelf in men's casual wear that may need some minor first aid."

chapter

30

Hormones

Few stressors can rival the power of hormones. Cigarette butts are what I use to gauge the severity of my mood swings these days. Mood swings, in case you've been out for a really long lunch, are one of the many joys of being female, forty-something, and at the mercy of fluctuating hormones. On the fun scale, mood swings rank right up there with trying on a swimsuit in front of a three-way mirror. Under fluorescent lights. While wearing knee-highs.

Enough pretty visuals, though: Back to how the cigarette-butt theory works. If I am in traffic and the driver in front of me flicks a cigarette butt out of his or her car and I *don't* have the urge to physically hurt the person, it is a good hormone day. It is a *great* hormone day. It is a day when I am in love with life.

I love my husband and my family and my house. I love the cracks in the driveway, the moss on the roof of the garage, and the adorable way the downspout has broken in two by the front walk. I even love cats, marigolds, and Barry Manilow, all of which I normally detest.

These hormones are so powerful that I can go to a

small-town Oktoberfest and observe a short and round couple in authentic German shorts with suspenders doing the polka and think they are cute. Cute, nothing. I adore them. I love them. I want to take them home and put them on the fireplace mantle. Obviously, a woman can never have enough good hormone days.

On the other end of the theory, if I am in traffic and the driver in front of me tosses out a cigarette butt and I want to lay on my horn, rip him out of his car, and make him crawl for two miles picking up cigarette butts and giving each and every one of them a dignified burial, I may be experiencing a slightly negative mood swing. These are days when I also must resist the urge to walk up behind young men whose pants are sagging and jerk those pants all the way to the ground. These also are the days when my children lock themselves in their rooms.

The problem with the hormones is that their swings are entirely unpredictable. One second, I want to live each moment to the fullest. I want to watch each autumn leaf drop to the ground. I want to learn to knit. I want to help Jerry Springer find good psychiatric counseling.

Two minutes later, the world is going to you-know-where in a handbasket and I loathe all of my kitchen appliances. Especially the mixer.

The next thing I know, my husband is agreeing with everything I say. Oh, maybe the world isn't so bad after all. My husband is nice and agreeable and—wait, why is he agreeing with me? Why? Because he's patronizing me! He never agrees with me! HOW DARE HE AGREE WITH ME!

And NOW someone has left an empty milk jug on the counter! Naturally, I call a family meeting to find out if I am the ONLY one who can see empty milk jugs. I am about to unleash domestic fury when the hormones do another crazy U-turn and—(sniff, sniff)—I realize I love them.

"Have I told you how blessed I am to be your mom? Your wife? Why don't we all just put our arms around each—"

"Watch it," one of them whispers, "she's got a wooden spoon behind her back."

That's exactly the kind of negativity I don't need. There's absolutely nothing wrong with me. Truthfully, I'm feeling quite stable right now. I am so in control and rational that I even know what to do to the next driver who flicks a cigarette butt onto the street.

Nuke 'em.

31

Metabolism
Slowdown

M other Nature has this entire food and metabolism
thing completely backward.

How is it a baby, who will eat anything from paper
napkins to potting soil, can burn nine thousand calories a
day just toddling around soaking diapers? Yet an adult,
who has a discriminating palate, works a full day, walks
ten miles a week, and does sit-ups during television commercials, gains weight by merely smelling banana bread?

I expand one pant size by walking into a chocolate store
and inhaling. I pack on two pounds minimum just carrying
a bowl of mashed potatoes from the stove to the table.

Where is the justice when a kid can eat an entire box of
high-fat macaroni and cheese with artificial color and
artificial flavor three times a week and burn it off before
you can say "naptime"? I had a delicious serving of
homemade macaroni and cheese three years ago and it's
still following me.

There is no justice, I tell you. Your average bird-leg
four-year-old has to be ordered to sit down and eat six
times during every meal. It's been decades since anybody

threatened to punish me for leaving the table. On several occasions I have been forcibly removed. Kicking and screaming.

I was never a permanent fixture in the kitchen as a child. Many days, the only time I went to the kitchen was when a large adult forced me. I could pick onions out of a meatloaf, conjure up a bad case of goose bumps over green beans, and make myself gag if there were tomatoes in the salad.

Still, I ate the better part of three squares a day, along with the usual cookies, pie, and ice cream, and never once worried about my weight. Today, each and every bite I swallow is washed down with anxiety about love handles, too much tummy, and corduroy pants making a loud swishing sound when I walk.

When I went away to college I lost seven pounds the first semester. I would forget to eat. Today, I never forget about food. I enjoy food. Tomatoes. Onions. Green beans. All of it. I enjoy shopping for it, cooking it, eating it, wrapping it up, storing it in the refrigerator, and starting the process all over again twenty minutes later. My tastebuds finally reach full maturity, and my metabolism has slowed to the speed of paste. Go figure.

In the last Miss America contest, a lean and leggy Miss Mississippi won the preliminary physical fitness competition. Asked how she prepared for the swimsuit parade, she said, "I have to eat a lot to keep weight on."

Millions of middle-aged women across America wanted to tweak her little button nose.

I was standing in line at the grocery store when I grabbed for a magazine promising to reveal the secret to boosting metabolism. The article said it was simple.

Double the amount you exercise and cut your food portions in half. It would be easier to take a sledge hammer to the bathroom scale than to reset my metabolism.

I have resigned myself to the fact that at this stage of life, the only time anyone will ever say I'm too thin for my own good will be when I'm so sick I won't even care. Get it on tape for me, will you?

The fact that we have a fast metabolism when we have little appreciation for food, and a slow metabolism when we have a great appreciation for food isn't fair; it just is.

In your twenties, you can lose five pounds in two days. In your thirties, you can lose five pounds in a week. Once you pass forty you can still lose five pounds, but they always keep finding you.

32

Pale in the Age
of Bronze

Sometimes I get a little stressed over the fact that I'm one of those pathetic people who don't tan. My skin color has two settings: pale and scorched. I can do Casper the Friendly Ghost or boiled lobster, but very few shades in between.

I'll go through the entire summer and come September I will still be as white as a sheet. I practically glow in the dark. On the upside, my family never needs to hunt for a flashlight. They just say, "Mom, show a little leg, Dad dropped the car keys."

Naturally, I am a marketer's dream when it comes to those self-tanning lotions. I first tried one in high school. The advertisement in *Teen* magazine said the lotion was guaranteed to transform my anemic-looking skin into a stunning beautiful bronze. My stunning bronzed skin would not only make me prettier, it would also make me more popular at the beach. What's more, I would look positively gorgeous dangling on the arm of an extremely handsome lifeguard.

I was excited. I was particularly excited because we

lived in the landlocked Midwest; I had never been to the beach and I was a rotten swimmer.

I slathered on the lotion. If one coat would make me bronze, two coats would make me very bronze. But why stop with very bronze? I slathered on more. I would aim for very, very bronze. After three thick, smelly coats of quick-tanning lotion, I climbed into bed with dreams of waking as a beautiful bronzed, tall, and blonde goddess. High hopes for a pale, short brunette, but a girl does expect a little something for a $5.95 investment.

I awoke the next morning and found the results were just like the bottle said—stunning. My brother took one look at me and was momentarily stunned, hitting his head as he fell backward laughing. My arms were the shade of a ripe peach. Add some fuzz and they could have plastered me on tourism brochures for the state of Georgia.

Then there were my legs. Stunning indeed. They were a sickening, putrid orange. My knee caps were the color of a jack-o'-lantern and the palms of my hands matched. My mother took one look, gasped, and ran to her medical book to check the symptoms for hepatitis.

For five days I wore blue jeans, a long-sleeved flannel shirt, shoes, socks and a wool scarf. A fine fashion ensemble, but it did draw a few stares in the ninety-degree July heat.

Last year I finally gathered the courage to try one of the new and improved tanning lotions that turn you lovely coffee brown, not a putrid, sickening orange. The lotion came in four shades: light brown, golden brown, dark brown, and extra crispy. Naturally, I went for the extra crispy. I applied the lotion with a steady circular motion and wound up with spots just like a cheetah.

Two weeks later I had another go at it. This time I tried a foam version of the self-tanning lotion and applied it with long vertical strokes per the directions. For six days I lived with stripes on the backs of my legs that bore a remarkable resemblance to a zebra.

We may live in the Age of Bronze, but I for one have made my peace being the color of paste.

33

In the Bag

Not until I was a parent did I truly come to understand the stress of going to school. All those worries about making new friends, fretting about finding the right bathroom in time, and wondering how hard the lessons would be and whether the teacher would be nice or crabby can be very frightening. Sometimes, the kids would get a little scared, too.

My greatest moment of apprehension was when the last one headed off to kindergarten. This was the child who refused to count past ten for me at home, but at her kindergarten interview, counted to thirty-five and was on her way to one hundred until the teacher stopped her. This was the child who had learned to read by studying the lyrics from a Randy Travis cassette tape. This was the child who, after much discussion and intense negotiations, finally agreed to go to kindergarten on one condition. Her demand, and I quote, was: "They better not make me sit by any yucky boys."

The big day came. I ushered her into her classroom, where the teacher had arranged desks facing one another in groups of four. We walked about the room looking for a name card that said "Melissa." It was in a cluster of four empty desks with three other name cards that said "Josh, Justin, and Matt." I looked at the name cards and then I looked at my baby in her little plaid skirt, Scotty dog shirt, red sneakers, and pigtails, and did what any sensible mother would have done. I bolted for the door.

Kids aside, there's someone else I always feel sorry for on the first day of school. It's not the kindergarten child riding the bus for the first time. And it's not the high school junior making a second pass at geometry. The person I feel the sorriest for on the first day of school is the mother who has decided to save a few bucks by packing school lunches all year.

Things go great in September. For four weeks she works off sheer adrenalin, pictures from *Martha Stewart Living* magazines, and an endless stream of healthy, creative sandwich fillings. Each day she faithfully packs fresh fruit, vegetable sticks, hearty sandwiches, and wholesome drinks. Some mornings she's so impressed with herself that she plays Guess What's in the Bag.

"Anyone want to guess what special treat is in their lunch?"

No response.

"Ants on a log!" she squeals. "That's right—celery with peanut butter and raisins!"

By October, the fun with food begins losing its edge, but she's still going strong. At least a couple of times a week she's still writing sweet little "thinking of you" notes on pretty pieces of paper and tucking clever little jokes and cartoons in the kids' lunches.

The routine, not unlike the Pita bread and onion

bagels, gradually grows stale, and by late October she secretly starts ticking off the days to Halloween. Milk chocolate in Snickers bars surely will count as a serving from the dairy food group.

Two weeks after Thanksgiving she's still trying to palm off dry turkey and stale pumpkin pie, saying, "You certainly can't buy this at the cafeteria window." (How right she is.) She herself suspects things may be heading south when one morning she throws a sixteen-ounce can of fruit cocktail into a lunch bag. Without a spoon. And without a can opener.

By December she's piling the grocery cart high with junk food she swore she would refuse to buy in the name of good nutrition and a better cash flow. Nacho-flavored pork rinds. Triple-decker oatmeal creme pies. Economy packs of bologna that aren't even all beef. She tells herself that lunches high in preservatives will boost the childrens' immunity systems.

February. It's been four months since she drew any of the kids' names in the shape of clouds on their paper lunch bags. Truth is it's been months since she used a paper lunch bag. Last week she used a plastic produce bag stamped "OPEN at this END." The week before that she set the entire cafeteria abuzz by sending a lunch in a small shopping bag from Victoria's Secret.

By April she is so sick of packing lunches that she starts an incentive plan. She will pay the kids a quarter if they pack their own lunches. She is seen sitting at the kitchen table with a cup of coffee saying, "Cold hot dogs are good for you. They'll help you with fractions," and "Yes, maraschino cherries ARE a fruit! Whoever said they weren't?"

By the end of May, when she has packed a school lunch consisting of Mountain Dew, a can of bacon-flavored Easy Cheese, and a pack of Ritz Crackers, there will be two things for which this worn and weary woman will be profoundly grateful: that an entire year of packing lunches is nearly over, and that nobody is grading her work.

34

Death, Taxes, and School Fundraisers

Benjamin Franklin said that only two things in life are certain—death and taxes. I'd like to add a third: school fundraisers.

If you are one of those rare birds who never have experienced the heartwarming joy of participating in a child's school fundraiser, e-mail me your address immediately. I'll send one of the kids right over.

For the past decade, we've peddled decorator candles, frozen lasagna, magazine subscriptions, entertainment coupon books, and fine-quality holiday gift wrap. We've sold everything under the sun, with the exception of men's hairpieces and large tropical reptiles.

Generally speaking, the kid who does best with the fundraiser is the one who has a parent who works for a large corporation and has a desk directly in the path of the elevator, the break room, or the restroom. All this parent has to do is set out the display box and wait for sales to roll in. But of course, when it comes to fundraisers, there's no such thing as a clean sale, which explains why one often hears conversations like the following:

"Look, I'll subscribe to *Better Homes and Gardens* if you'll buy three pecan logs and a tin of butter toffee."

"Great, but that means my kid is still one subscription shy of goal, which means she won't get her incentive T-shirt or the 100 percent genuine plastic key ring. Can't you go for a *Popular Mechanics*, too?"

"Fine. I'll take another magazine if you'll split a deluxe five-pound variety fudge box with Joe, who's selling yellow trash bags." And so the sales continue like one never-ending bad chain letter, all for the good of playground equipment, pom-poms, science labs, and baseball jerseys.

For the past seven months, we have helped a certain eighth-grade student shamelessly hawk candy bars to help fund a class trip to Washington, D.C. What red-blooded American wouldn't flood the city with chocolate in exchange for their child being able to visit the highest court in the land and survey the official residence of the president? We know our child is excited about this educational opportunity, too, because we hear her talking about it with her friends almost daily.

"Did you hear what they said in history? Yes! We're taking TWO buses and the hotel has a POOL! That is so cool."

What's forcing friends and neighbors to buy twelve dozen Twizzlers and a couple of cases of Snickers in exchange for our kid having the opportunity to stand in the the magnificent Jefferson Memorial?

"They said one night will be All Girl Swim and then All Boy Swim and the next night will be Boy AND Girl Swim!"

Sure, my husband's co-workers blame him for their mid-afternoon candy bar addiction, my parents leave their wallets in the car when they visit now, and once-friendly neighbors have pulled the shades and bolted the doors, but we don't regret a single candy bar, because we hear the excitement of American history resonating in her voice.

"Most of our lunches will be at a food court or in a mall, and the sponsor said we might get to mill around a little bit and shop and we're to stay with someone at all times."

Seven-hundred sixty-eight candy bars, ninety-eight thousand grams of fat and 134 billion calories. Every bit of it, most certainly, for a good, educational cause.

35

Walk a Mile in
My Platforms

Let me be the first to suggest that girls who wear platform shoes should carry liability insurance. You simply
can't wear shoes that lift you beyond the pull of gravity
and not encounter serious health hazards. You fall from
that kind of altitude and you're looking at sprained ankles,
broken wrists, and blackouts from the rapid increase in air
pressure.

If I wore the platform shoes my daughters wear, I'd be
nursing a nosebleed within five seconds.

"Those tall platform shoes worry me," I tell the
youngest.

"These shoes are fine," she responds, strapping on a pair
that push her into the 160th percentile on the height chart
for fourteen-year-old girls.

"What's to worry about?" she asks.

"Your safety," I answer.

"These shoes are very safe," she says, teetering over to
the refrigerator.

"I'd like to see you come home from the store and lug
ten bags of groceries up a flight of stairs in those shoes and

tell me they're safe," I say.

"I would, Mom, but our kitchen is on the ground floor."

"Well, I worry that you can't run in platforms," I say.

Both girls now are in the kitchen, wearing shoes that could double as stilts, laughing their heads off.

"Why would we need to run?" they squeal.

Am I the only one around here who can answer the obvious? "You might need to run in case a dog comes charging at you!" I say. "In case of a fire! In case of a clearance sale!"

Both girls tell me I am overreacting and am completely off base. They are right. I know they are right, because five seconds later I watch the oldest, who is not running but standing perfectly still, turn on the television. One second she's upright, the next second she has toppled off her platforms at a perfect right angle.

I have all but given up the line of argument about sensible shoes. It's futile because the word "sensible" is relative.

When I wore wooden clogs in the '70s, my Great Aunt Mary asked why I didn't get some sensible shoes. Naturally, she meant a sensible pair like hers—sturdy brown lace-up jobs with two-inch block heels. They were durable, all-purpose shoes, ideal for trekking through blizzards, stomping grasshoppers, or building log cabins on the Nebraska prairie. They were so sensible I wouldn't have been caught dead in them.

Sensible shoes for my mother's generation were the little black flats. With the exception of Mary Tyler Moore, those sensible shoes made every woman's thighs look ten pounds heavier and eight inches wider.

Sensible for my generation has been the tennis shoe. The bulk of my fashionable dress shoes took up residence in boxes on the closet shelf years ago. They bear labels like: chestnut brown pumps (cause corns); strappy black heels (generate shin splints); and navy heels (cut into ankles). Most women my age slid into ugly, clunky sports shoes when we became pregnant or found ourselves on our feet all day. Sensible never looked so bad and felt so good.

My son brought a female friend to the house last week. She was wearing a short black skirt with Army surplus combat boots. What could I say?

"Nice to meet you. What sensible shoes."

36

Billy

You have not truly experienced stress unless you have been the parent of a dawdler and dreamer. These are the children who simultaneously cause moms and dads head-banging frustration and button-busting pride. They also prompt parents to write letters like the following to school administrators:

Dear Superintendent,

I hereby request my son's name be changed to Billy on his permanent record. You know Billy. He's the boy in the **Family Circus** cartoons who can't get off the school bus and go home without making 125 detours.

This may be an odd request, but permit me to explain. Moments ago, I finished my 3,925th lecture to my child on how important it is to try his hardest in school.

Energized by our little pep talk, he was on his way to more thoughtful, analytical essays, better grades, and honor roll with distinction. His books were in sight on his desk, only a few feet away. Beside the desk lay an inner tube that had not been inflated for five months.

My most recent speech, containing the often-repeated refrain, "There's no time like the present," rang loudly in his ears. He looked at his books; he looked at the inner tube. Then he did what he knew he should have done at the beginning of the grading period: He grabbed a hand pump and began to slowly pump up the inner tube.

While he was busy pumping, his eyes wandered about the room. He observed a pencil with a broken point by his textbook. He heard another familiar phrase resounding in his head: "Be prepared, plan ahead."

Obedient to the voice within, he traipsed downstairs to the kitchen and rummaged through the junk drawer, where he counted four other pencils with broken points, sixteen loose paper clips, a dead nine-volt battery, and a small pencil sharpener shaped like an Army tank. He took the sharpener back to his room, sat down by the trash can, and proceeded to sharpen the pencil. And sharpen and sharpen and sharpen. By final calculations, the unbroken pencil shaving was at least eleven inches in length, a personal best.

Satisfied, he once again headed to the desk, where he would surely become one of the best students in his class (possibly valedictorian by the time he finished his senior year). But his foot caught on something. A book. He heard another phrase from the lecture: "Finish what you start." He opened the book to the page with the folded ear and proceeded to read. *Dracula*. Poetry is part of the school literature experience; *Dracula* is not. Poetry was on the desk.

Ah yes, the desk. *Dracula* drew to a close, and once again our scholar attempted to make his way to his desk. Right after a brief detour to the bathroom. The sound of something heavy was heard scraping across the tile floor upstairs. I rapped on the door to see what was the commotion. The bathroom window was open wide, the screen was off, and a telescope was trained on a bright star in the northern sky.

You can see, sir, why we would like to have the boy's name changed to Billy on his permanent record. Billy is not the name we chose for him at birth, but somehow it is a more accurate reflection of who he is. He has every intention of excelling at school, just as Billy has every intention of going straight home after stepping off the bus. And he will excel, slowly but surely, just like Billy reaches his front door—after 287.5 billion fascinating side trips, distractions, and detours.

Sincerely,

Billy's Mom

37

The View
from There

There are days when the most stressful thing a mother can do is look at herself from her child's perspective.

Infants see mothers as a generous milk supply and an endless source of dry diapers—a home-delivery quick mart that never closes—open nights, weekends, and holidays.

Toddlers see mothers as giant stop signs: *Stop pushing the buttons on the VCR. Stop blowing bubbles in your milk. Stop stuffing ladybugs in your pockets. Stop pulling the dog's ears.*

Preschool children see mothers as tall people obsessed with sleep and beds: *It's time for bed. Goodnight, and don't get out of bed. It's still early—stay in bed. It's time for naps; go lie down on your bed.* Strange thing is, the kids aren't tired. It's mom who falls asleep on the couch, nods off reading *Curious George*, and dozes with her head on their pillows listening to night-time prayers.

The elementary school child sees mom as a border crossing guard: *Do you have your lunch? Did you clean your ears? Did you hang up your towel? Did you brush your teeth? Do you have your homework finished?*

The middle school child often sees Mom as, well, embarrassing. She not only sings along with the oldies station on the radio, she refuses to keep her distance at the mall and picks restaurants where the lighting is so bright the entire family runs the risk of being seen together.

To the full-fledged teen, mom has never fully let go of that border crossing guard persona. Which explains why she now has evolved into a card-carrying, surveillance-trained FBI agent: *Whose house is the party at? Will parents be home? Do the parents seem normal? How do you define "normal"? Do you think there will be alcohol or drugs? What if there IS alcohol or drugs? Who else will be there? Who's driving? What time will you be home?*

The older the kids get, the tougher a mom can seem. She talks too much, pries without a trace of subtlety, listens too intently, and scrutinizes events with a vigilance J. Edgar Hoover would have envied.

The older mom gets, the tougher the kids seem. One minute, she gazes into the face of a child and sees a look that says: Hey, you're all right, mom. Thirty seconds later, she faces an exasperated grimace that demands to know if anything *ever* gets by her. (Answer: Only when she sleeps, and even then she keeps one eye open.)

I recently saw a friend who is the mother of two teenage sons. She said her boys have taken to calling her Smother. Funny. At least the boys think so.

Why bother with all the questions, supervision, limits, and standards? Why not just sit back and let 'em do their own thing? Turn 'em loose as soon as they can catch a ride to the mall, let 'em go to every movie "all the other kids are seeing." Let 'em watch cable 'til their eyes bulge. Let 'em hang out who knows where until sunrise. It would sure make some days a whole lot more pleasant.

I don't know a single mother who likes playing the shrew or being cast in the role of bad guy. So why do we do it? Because we have to. It says so in the Motherhood Manual: Volume 2, page 347, paragraph 5.

Oh yes, one other tiny reason mothers stick their noses into their children's lives.

Love.

38

Dinner: Be There
or Be Square

This week, we are striving to attain a challenging goal that we have not attempted in a very long time—having dinner together.

Next to nailing a fried egg to a tree, nothing may be more difficult than rounding up three teenagers and two adults for a shared meal. Dictators have overthrown governments in small Caribbean countries with less effort than it takes to get five of us around the dinner table.

"How does Wednesday night look for you?" I ask the better half.

"Wednesday, Monday, and Friday are bad, but the third Tuesday of next month is good."

"Tuesday's out," yells a voice from the around the corner. "Softball practice and orchestra rehearsal."

"Let's go for Thursday," I suggest.

"Thursday's good for me, as long as we're through eating by 4:30," says a pair of legs hanging out of the refrigerator. "I have to be to the library by 5 for a group project on the disintegrating American family."

"How about Friday?" is only halfway out of my mouth when "concert" and "baby-sitting" are fired at me from opposite ends of the house.

We can manage dinner for three about 60 percent of the time, and dinner for four about 40 percent of the time, but dinner for five carries the type of odds that cause bookies to suffer male pattern baldness. Hard to believe rounding the five of us up was once as easy as standing in the kitchen, opening a cardboard box, and yelling, "Pizza!"

We used to be able to have dinner together a lot. Of course, we also used to be able to split one Happy Meal between the three kids, and their primary means of transportation was an old red wagon. Believe me, it is much harder to pluck a kid out of a car pointed in the direction of the mall than to pull her off a Barbie Big Wheel and haul her into the house for dinner.

Mothers will tell you that dinner with the family is a fundamental maternal need right up there with a strong disinfectant and a good bubble bath. Mothers need those occasional golden moments when every chair is occupied, feet crowd under the table, dishes clatter, salad and green beans are passed in opposite directions, and there is a clamor for extra napkins. To a mother, dinner is a commotion of sheer delight.

Be warned that this is not a need that passes with time. Grandmothers are legendary for getting aggressive about having the entire family for a meal. On several occasions, I have been forced to commit to large family dinners at Mom's under the threat of a meat fork and butter knife.

As the count stands now, three will be here at home for grub on Monday and Wednesday, two on Tuesday, four on Thursday, and Friday and Saturday are up in the air.

"That settles it," I announce. "I'm putting a hold on Saturday night, six o'clock. No excuses."

"Sounds more like a threat than an invitation," someone observes.

"Take it anyway you want," I say, picking up a spatula. "Just be here."

The Art of Chaos

When you have three teens in the house, you could put in a full forty-hour week doing nothing but crisis management.

This morning it was an allergic reaction to the contact lens cleaning solution. Yesterday it was a personal breakdown regarding a chapter on physiology. The day before that, it was a heated discussion over an unchaperoned camping trip and the meaning of the word "trust." Two days before that it was a dislocated kneecap.

So much chaos, so little time.

When you put it all in perspective, I would have to say that today's mother-son discussion on tattoos went quite well.

I am behind the wheel of the car and the high school junior is in the passenger seat when he suddenly asks what I think about tattoos.

"Why, are you joining the Merchant Marine?" I quiz.

"No."

"The circus?" I ask.

"No."

"If you're not shipping out and you haven't signed with

Barnum and Bailey, why are you asking about tattoos?"

"Don't get so excited," he says, inching as close as possible to the passenger door. "I didn't say I wanted one. I just want to know what you think about them."

"I think they're fine," I snap. "I have absolutely no objection whatsoever to those press-on tattoos in the Cracker Jack boxes."

"C'mon," he says, rolling his eyes, "what do you think about real tattoos? Not that I'd get one, because you have to be eighteen to get one without parental permission and I'm only seventeen—until six months, four days, two hours, and thirty seconds from now."

"I've got a better question. What do you think about tattoos?" I quiz, boring holes into the side of his head with my beady eyes.

"I think they're okay, if they're small," he says, matter-of-factly.

"Define small," I say, feeling a little faint as I straighten out the wheels, mere seconds before careening across the median.

"Nothing bigger than four inches by four inches," he says confidently.

"So you're thinking of something ugly, garish, and permanent that is roughly the size of Mount Rushmore?"

No response.

I calmly remind him of a twenty-something family friend who recently got a "small" tattoo.

"He's a really buff guy, and you might think that tattoo covering his entire upper chest may look impressive now. But mark my words, thirty years from now he's going to be more bloat than buff. Do you know what's going to happen to that tattoo then?" I ask.

"No, but you're gonna tell me, aren't you?"

"That huge snake will sag right along with everything else on that guy. It will slither south, lose all shape and definition, and be a big black-and-blue blob highlighting his pot belly."

"Maybe the guy will stay buff all his life," my son offers.

"Maybe. And maybe I'll become a swimsuit model tomorrow."

"Lots of kids at school have tattoos."

"You're not lots of kids," I snap.

"Hey, even Barbie has a tattoo."

"Yeah, and Barbie also has big bosoms and dates a guy named Ken. We're not about to let you do those things either," I say, screeching to a halt as the light turns yellow.

Realizing that I may be getting a little intense—and wishing to get back on the pavement, as opposed to continue driving on the shoulder of the road—I commence deep breathing and ask if I have come on too strong on the subject of tattoos.

"No stronger than you came on about motorcycles," he says, yawning.

"Refresh me," I say.

"You said if I ever got a death-trap motorcycle, you'd hunt it down and slash the tires."

"Okay, so I don't like to be vague on these issues. I detest ambiguity. Is that a sin?"

"Not at all. I was just wondering what you thought," he says.

"Well, now you know."

"Want to discuss body piercing?" he asks, tilting back his seat and closing his eyes.

"Depends," I answer. "Do you want me to keep this car on the road?"

chapter

40

The Hang Up

Let me just say I know that life sometimes can be hard for teenage girls. Trust me. Been there, done that, got the T-shirt.

I know memorizing the stages of cell development for biology can be hard. I know finding pants that fit just right can be hard. I know that making curly hair straight and making straight hair curly can be hard. I know that painting toenails and fitting in with a circle of friends can be hard.

Naturally, I figured the things that were hard when I was a teenage girl would be hard for girls today. What I never in my wildest dreams anticipated being hard for any teenage girl is the simple act of hanging up the phone.

For most of the world, this is an uncomplicated process. As you sense the conversation drawing to a close, your brain retrieves an immensely witty and creative phrase from the memory bank like, "Bye," "Buh-Bye," or "Talk to you later." A brief but polite salutation is followed by a succinct CLICK.

For certain adolescent girls, however, hanging up the phone is hard. Very hard.

Witness the following:

Girl A has been talking to Girl B on the phone for twenty minutes. Having run out of things to say, Girl A is heard to say, "Okay, let's hang up now."

Such a statement causes pulsing sensations in the index fingers of those lurking near the phone, hoping to push buttons on the numerical key pad and make a few calls themselves. Hopes are dashed, however, when Girl A continues, "Do you want to hang up first, or should I hang up first?"

Now, you can't hear what Girl B says, but it doesn't matter what Girl B says, because it is apparent from Girl A's end of the conversation that both girls are in a quandary over who will hang up first. Like pondering hairstyles, shoes, and which shade of lip gloss to buy, one of the hallmarks of adolescence is that it is a period of life marked by indecision. I want to go to the party. I don't want to go to the party. I like the double-ear pierce. I don't like the double-ear pierce. Leonardo is cool. Leonardo is not cool. Berry Berry is my shade. Sweet Honey is my shade.

After a back-and-forth volley equal in length to the entire Wimbledon tennis tournament, Girl A says, "Okay then, let's hang up together. On the count of three. Ready?"

Surging with adrenalin, Girl A edges close to the phone base, then slowly and deliberately begins counting, "One . . . two . . . three."

On the count of three, however, the receiver is still frozen to her ear. Without so much as drawing a breath, she whispers, "Are you there?" She then explodes with amazement and screams, "I'M STILL HERE, TOO!!! Tee, hee, hee, hee!" and wild, maniacal laughter ricochets off the walls.

Then, using one of the most dreaded phrases to cross the lips of an adolescent female in possession of a phone, Girl A says, "Okay, let's try it again. Ready? On the count of three. One, two . . . "

Basic economics, conjugating French verbs, walking in platform shoes, and coping with blemishes, I anticipated would be hard. But simply hanging up the phone? Never.

41

Driven to Prayer

We have a family history of hostility when it comes to teaching one another to drive stick shifts. When my grandfather taught my mother to drive a manual, he said, "Get in and start the motor." She did. She then let the clutch out too quickly and killed it. He said, "*%#&$!!@! Get out!"

It was the world's shortest driving lesson.

My husband and I bought our first stick shift as newlyweds. The car salesman said it would save us four hundred dollars on the sticker price. We believed him. He said the car would last three times longer than an automatic. We believed that, too. He then said we could learn to drive a stick shift with just one quick trip around the parking lot. Did I mention that we were young and extremely naive?

We lurched and lunged our way home from the dealership, killing the engine at four-way stops, popping the clutch at traffic lights, and provoking numerous hand gestures from fellow motorists whizzing by.

The next morning we tested the bonds of friendship by

asking our neighbor to teach us to drive a stick. Under his tutelage, we lurched and lunged and snapped our necks for nearly forty-five minutes in an empty stadium parking lot, trying to get into first gear. Miraculously, we remain friends, although he now has a pathological aversion to recliner chairs that throw him upright with a sudden thrust.

Last week, our hunt for a used truck our son could use for his mowing jobs came to and end when we found a real beauty. Sixty-five thousand miles, cracked windshield, rusted muffler, definite pull to the left, and a panel light that continually glows "check engine." Oh yes, and a five-speed manual transmission.

I did my stint as driving instructor two nights ago. Like any victim of trauma, I have blocked most of the experience from memory. However, I do remember lurching and pitching about the subdivision like a crazed jackrabbit dodging bullet fire. I also remember the high point of our session being when my son looked at me and said, "The way you're yelling, why don't you just hit me?" I punched him in his upper arm.

I remember one more thing—praying. Lots of praying.

"Dear Lord, I thank you that the '93 Ford F150s were not equipped with air bags, as I know this one would have deployed long ago, breaking both my arms and unmercifully smashing me against the cab of this truck."

We lurched and pitched and reeled for what seemed like hours with our heads and upper bodies snapping forward, jerking backward, then thrusting forward again.

"Heavenly Father, I pray that you would protect my face. I know it's not a lot, but in the throes of middle

age, it's better than most of what follows from the neck down."

After only two driving sessions, our son has now mastered the fine art of shifting. What's more, the whiplash my husband and I have suffered is improving daily, and the night terrors only come between two and three o'clock in the morning.

Despite such a pleasant, happy ending, however, I will never again relax in a recliner chair as long as I live.

42

My Parents
Never

When grandparents agree to come from out of state and watch three kids so you and your husband can get away for a long weekend, you naturally expect that there may be a small wave of rebellion. You just don't expect it to come from the grandparents.

What's the matter with grandparents today? I left lengthy lists they ignored, detailed instructions they disregarded, a daily itinerary they refused to follow, and a long list of emergency phone numbers they never once clutched to their chests in a state of panic.

I stocked groceries, planned meals, and gave a thorough tour of the kitchen cabinets, showing them where every ingredient stood eagerly waiting. What did they do five minutes after my husband and I backed out of the driveway? They took a vote on who wanted to close the kitchen. It was unanimous. They ate out for four days.

My parents *never* would have done something like that when I was a kid.

Before my husband and I left, we pointed out a few houses Grandma and Grandpa should visit that weekend during the neighborhood's annual garage sales. They did as they were told. Then they went back to our house and did something else. They rolled our decrepit, rotting patio table into the driveway and stuck a sign on it that said "$35." When nobody expressed any interest, they changed the sign to "Best Offer." When still nobody expressed any interest, they chopped up the table and stuffed the wood in cardboard boxes for the trash pick-up.

My parents never would have done something like that when I was a kid.

After they finished with the ax and saw, they went out and splurged on a nice patio table and chairs—big, comfy chairs that you can get in and out of safely. They're nothing like the old, little wooden benches, where you had to warn the fella sitting on the other end that you were standing up or he would suddenly find himself scooting derrier-first across the concrete patio. They even bought an umbrella to go with the table.

Who ARE these people?

I'm telling you, my parents NEVER would have done something like that when I was a kid.

While my husband and I were touring scenic sites four states away, my parents were joking around like they were teenagers and playing games with tortilla chips. They ran sprints in the backyard and chased one of the kids around the block on a bicycle. They even took the girls to the mall and gleefully killed time wandering through boutiques and stores examining toe rings and glitter nail polish.

My parents NEVER would have done something like that when I was a kid. Does ANYONE believe me? No one will ever again believe me when I say my folks were tow-the-line, let's-finish-up-those-leftovers, no-nonsense, a-penny-saved-is-a-penny-earned people.

I overheard one of the kids recapping her four glorious days with Grandma and Grandpa for a friend on the phone. What especially caught my ear was the tail end of her weekend narrative. She said, "Yeah, they are cool. My parents NEVER would have done something like that!"

43

Stranger Danger

Mom has been going against her own wise motherly advice she gave me as a child. Yes, Mom has been talking to strangers.

It doesn't seem to matter who they are, or where they are; there she is just chatting away with virtual strangers (e.g., the sales clerk working in casual weekend wear) like she's known them all of her life. Actually, Mom tells me, that's not possible because the sales clerk just moved to town in April. The clerk made the cross-country move after she'd gone to visit a friend who was stationed at a naval base in Maryland, and later found out that while she was gone her husband—correction: make that her "stinkin' husband"—had been carrying on with a twenty-two-year-old aerobics instructor.

Mom can get more information from a stranger in two minutes than Barbara Walters can squeeze out of an hour-long *20/20* interview. The problem is, Mom is not a professional journalist like Barbara. She's a professional grandma. So the question is, should grandmas go around striking up conversations with strangers?

Mom and Dad recently returned from a trip to San Francisco that the family gave them for their fiftieth wedding anniversary. By their second day at the hotel, Mom knew that the young man working the front desk was from the Philippines. She also knew that he had a brother in San Francisco, a brother in the Netherlands, a brother in Australia, and a sister in Michigan. The sister in Michigan doesn't have kids, and that seems to be where the mother goes to visit once a year when she comes from the Philippines.

I listened as she relayed the family tree of the hotel clerk, and then I said, "Mom, how do you get such personal information just checking into a hotel?"

"What's personal?" she says. "We weren't personal, we were just polite."

As part of the package, Mom and Dad took a hot-air balloon ride over the Napa Valley. They discovered one of the other passengers also was from Kansas City—small world and all that—and at one time had even worked at the same university Mom and Dad had. By the time the flight was over, the balloon pilot said if he could remember some names, he was sure he could blackmail all three of them.

(The pilot, in case you were wondering, got his commercial balloon pilot license in 1981 and was part of an archaeological dig in Egypt with the University of California. Dad says the pilot has also flown over dig sites in Kenya, Africa, and France. At home, he enjoys wine making and running marathons. And, oh yes, he also works as a high school track coach. Ten more minutes in the hot-air balloon and Mom and Dad would have known the guy's shirt size.)

When pressed on the matter of talking to strangers, Mom snaps a frosty comeback: "It's your father's fault." She claims that ever since Dad started losing his hair, he never leaves home without wearing a bill cap from his collection of thirty or more. "So we go somewhere," Mom explains, "and he's wearing a hat that says, for instance, Branson. People come up and say, 'Oh are you from Branson?' Naturally, we have to explain that we're *not* from Branson and, well, surely you understand."

"I'm trying, Mom. I'm trying."

"Well, what do you expect us to do? Just walk away and let them believe we're from *Branson*?"

"No, Mom, of course not."

The kids have seen their grandma in action, too. Once they were at the fabric store with her when she got into a long conversation with a gentleman and his wife about the popularity of sunflowers. When Mom began expressing considerable dismay that the couple did not know Kansas was the Sunflower State, the kids ran away and hid behind the notions rack.

So what's a daughter to do? Lay down the law to Mom? Take away her Fox News Channel privileges? Threaten to mess up her Medicare file? I choose to talk.

"Listen, Mom, you know when the kids were little, we told them never to talk to a stranger unless the stranger knew the secret password, which was broccoli soup and salad."

"Your father and I have a password," she says.

"What?"

"Retired. It means we've got the time to talk to anybody we want about whatever we want."

"Fine, Mom. But listen, you know to be sensible, right?" I ask.

"What?" she says, bristling like I had just spilled cherry Jell-O on her light gray carpet. "You think I'd take candy from a stranger and get in a car?"

"Don't be silly. I know you're not going to take candy from a stranger, unless it's a high-grade premium milk chocolate—and then I'd have reason to worry."

"You should," she said, whipping out a small Ghirardelli milk chocolate bar from her purse.

I give up. I can't control her. I can only offer my advice. If she doesn't take it, that's her business.

The irony of all this is that yesterday morning I was waiting in line at the bank, standing next to a woman with five-year-old twin boys (no fertility drugs, born four weeks premature, but fine after only two weeks in NICU) and it turns out her mother, Betty Jo, who lived in Texas but retired to Phoenix and loves drying and pressing wild-flowers, does the exact same thing—talks to perfect strangers all the time.

Wacky. Absolutely wacky.

44

Touchdown Momma

Since Mom lives five hundred miles away and doesn't get over too often, she thought it would be nice if we did something special together as mother and daughter on her most recent visit. Spend a little time together.

Connect.

Relate.

Sit on the couch and watch pro football.

"You're kidding," I said.

"No, now sit down and don't talk so loud. I can't hear the starting lineup."

I envisioned Mom doing a lot of things once she retired. Doting on five grandchildren. Reading. Gardening. Helping older neighbors. The fact that I never anticipated she would become a crazed football fanatic was sheer oversight on my part.

So this red team is playing this blue team and all of a sudden Mom starts chattering away about Wade Phillips, some irksome little man, she says, who is forever hopping up and down in a red stocking cap.

I'm sitting there thinking to myself, Wade Phillips,

Wade Phillips. Hmmm. Maybe she's talking about someone on Dad's side of the family.

"He's the coach for the Bills!" she huffs in exasperation. "Where have you been?"

I don't know, Mom. Parenting? Working? Cleaning the bathroom?

I soon learn the great thing about watching football with Mom is that she makes comments the network guys only dream about making. Comments like:

"I hate him!"

"Now there's a lineman who had a big dinner. It's a wonder he can bend over."

"If I made a bad play like that, I'd just lay there, too."

"That player weighs three hundred pounds. You know, when you're that big, you really do need a hand up."

She looks like Mom. She sounds like Mom. But how can this be the same woman who used to chug a five-minute cup of hot coffee in twenty seconds because there were people to see, places to go, and things to do—now sitting for hours at a time following football?

"Okay! Now's your chance," she says.

"What's my chance, Mom? To go for pretzels, to send out for some of those buffalo wings?" I say.

"Not you," she snaps. "I'm talking to the quarterback."

Great. She doesn't just talk about the players, she talks to the players.

Five seconds later, my jaw drops another four inches when she says, "I like that referee. He's new."

"You know the refs, Mom?"

"Oh, sure," she says. "This is his first season. He's very good. Some are slow, but he calls the plays right away.

"Look," she yells. "They're going for the head in the box."

Sure enough, a ref walks over to a box and sticks his head in, apparently to watch a play.

"They rarely overturn the play when they do that, but this is interesting," she continues, never missing a beat.

The game heats back up and the kids, who usually don't watch football, pass through the room and stop dead in their tracks when they see Grandma thrust both arms high in the air. They look at her, and she looks back and yells, "TOUCHDOWN! Haven't your parents taught you anything?"

The game resumes and so does she.

"You know, they have classes for dumb women who don't understand the rules," she says.

"What's that?" I say.

"They have classes for people who don't understand football. Would you believe there are people who don't even know why they punt or kick, or how many downs there are?"

"Shocking," I whisper, all the while quietly hoping that her steady commentary will eclipse my conspicuous silence.

"The Buffalo coach shows no emotion. I like the Steelers' coach," she says. "That guy has some emotion. Now, see that pinch-faced white-haired guy on the side-line? Him I don't care for. See the player at the far right of the screen? He played one game with a broken bone. Always has his mouth going."

The rapid-fire football commentary has left me stunned. This is the same woman who just yesterday took me aside and told me the upstairs bathroom would look a lot better if I would take the time to fold the edges on the guest towels under from both sides, instead of folding them in half and exposing the selvages.

During a commercial break, she calmly announces that she does not like Troy Aikman, quarterback for Dallas.

"You did know he quarterbacks for Dallas, didn't you?" she asks. Clearly, what she really wanted to do was rap on my skull and say, "Hello? Anybody home?"

"You know, he courted Lorrie Morgan for a while and couldn't put up with her child."

I was about to make a profound statement like, "What a jerk," when she continued—

"Of course, I don't like Lorrie Morgan either. She was going around for a while with Fred Thompson, the senator from Tennessee, if you can picture that."

Football, country music, and politics, all in one sitting. This is unbelievable mother-daughter bonding.

It was a nice afternoon until Mom found out the Kansas City Chiefs' game wasn't being televised in Indianapolis. Mom, who has never surfed the Net and has for years staunchly resisted our suggestion to buy a personal computer, suddenly insists that we try to find the game on the Internet. "I think the NFL has a Web site," she says. "You can find it, can't you? Maybe we should get one of the kids. Won't that screen come up any faster?"

I find the NFL Web site and sure enough, they are posting the scores of all the teams playing that afternoon. I show Mom how to use the mouse and hit the refresh button to update the scores, when I hear her tell Dad, "Maybe it's time we get one of these things."

The game wasn't the same on the Web as it would have been on TV. Somewhere at the end of the first quarter, Mom lost interest. Other than getting agitated and threatening to call the television station, she took it pretty well. "If I'd known they weren't going to televise the Chiefs, I'd have gone home this morning."

chapter

45

The Sandwich Generation: Make Mine "To Go"

M y mother has mailed me two newspaper clippings with a Post-it note stuck to the front of them. The first clipping tells the story of a woman in England who left her mother lying on the floor of their home for a week, even vacuuming around her, because the mother "often collapsed and remained on the floor for several days." The second clipping is a story about a man who barricaded his ninety-two-year-old grandmother in his basement.

On the pink floral Post-it accompanying the clippings, Mom has written, "What are your plans for us?"

Mom's dark sense of humor is part of what makes her a survivor. This is her way of reminding me of yet another contemporary source of stress: the fact that I may one day be a member of the Sandwich Generation—that growing demographic of people who simultaneously care for aging parents and children. But I don't think Mom and Dad are going to need our attention for a while.

When they retired, we figured they would do what all retired people do: slow down, smell the roses, get a van, and poke around the country wearing sweatshirts that say, "We're spending our kids' inheritance."

Not today's retirees. A lot of them have somehow managed to ratchet the leisurely pace of the golden years up to a speed of Mach 2. My parents are constantly on the move, continually scanning the horizon for what they refer to as "a little project."

"I like a little project," says Mom.

"Having a little project is good," says Dad.

Lest you get the wrong idea, they're not talking about knitting or cross-pollinating petunias. To them, a little project is taking a tractor and trailer, picking up sixteen tons of crushed stone at a nearby rock quarry, and shoveling it onto my brother's dirt driveway while he is at work. Just typical little projects for retirees in the sixty-to-seventy age bracket.

Last spring, when they caught wind that my husband and I were stripping wallpaper and getting ready to paint, they packed an overnight bag and zipped over five hundred "it's not that many" miles because they like a little project.

We started painting at 8:30 A.M. By 8:35, my mother pronounced the ladder unsafe. Ten seconds later, Mom and I were speeding to the hardware store. I had to yell at her to stay in the car until the vehicle came to a complete stop. She was out the door and in the paint aisle before I had the keys out of the ignition.

In the three minutes we were gone, my dad rerouted a heating vent, shored up the wooden framework around the crawl space, and staked out a twenty-by-forty-foot section of the backyard for a small garden. Fortunately, we were back before he had worked his way out to the shed, where we keep the chainsaw and an eight-pound sledgehammer.

So much for the myth that retirees slow their pace and stick close to home—except for Wednesdays, when the Day-Old Bread Shop has senior citizen discount day.

During a brief lull in the frenzied painting project, Mom read a wire story in our Indianapolis paper about a cattle drive that happened two days before in downtown Kansas City. She announced that the reporter had the story all wrong.

"How do you know the story is wrong?" I asked.

"The story says the cattle ambled," she said.

"How do you know the cattle didn't amble?"

"We were there. The cattle ran. They were Texas long-horns, and it was a stampede."

"Mom, it makes me nervous when I hear you and Dad do things like that."

"What do you think we are? Nuts?" she exclaimed. "We moved to higher ground when we saw cattle coming toward us on the side streets."

"Thank goodness," I sighed.

"You bet. We dashed up to the fourth story of a parking garage. We had a great view of the paramedics working on a cowboy who injured his ankle after his horse slipped and fell."

I thought retirees napped in the afternoons, sat with an afghan over their legs by the fire in the winter, sipped lemonade in the summer, and worked on honest-to-goodness little projects like jigsaw puzzles and crosswords.

If these two are any indication of how the senior set is kicking back these days, I'll need the next twenty-five years to get up to speed.

But hey, it's always good to have a little project.

One time, when I spoke at a fundraiser, some of the key organizers were getting together for lunch. There were to be seven ladies, but only six were present. Questions started flying; "Where's Joyce?"

"Who knows," another answered. "On Tuesdays, she volunteers at the Crisis Pregnancy Center."

"On Thursdays she volunteers at the school," chimed in another.

Someone else said, "Well, this is Wednesday. You think she goes somewhere on Wednesdays?"

An exasperated voice said, "Hey, she's retired. You can bet she's out somewhere. Those people are *never* home."

We call my parents the Minute Men. They keep the gas tank full and leave their shoes pointed toward the garage when they go to bed, just in case they should get a phone call or invitation during the night. Be it for a wedding, funeral, birth, or cheese and crackers celebrating the vernal equinox, these folks can be ready to go with three changes of clothes, a thermos of hot coffee, and an appropriate hostess gift in a New York minute.

Not all retirees act like the Minute Men. My eighty-nine-year-old father-in-law doesn't back the car out of the garage until he checks the Weather Channel. Repeatedly. If he is planning the 112-mile drive to our house, he first checks with the Weather Channel. Then he calls us to verify the accuracy of the Weather Channel.

"What's the temperature over there?" he asks.

"Fifty-four."

"The Weather Channel says it's fifty-six."

"It's sunny right now," my husband says.

"Sunny to partly cloudy, with a 20 percent chance of

showers," my father-in-law corrects. "There's a cold front in Wyoming and it's raining in Florida, but I think it's okay for the trip."

He will continue checking the Weather Channel until the moment before departure, noting any and all weather changes from the San Fernando Valley to the Upper Michigan Peninsula. If, heaven forbid, he has to use the facilities before leaving, he will again check the Weather Channel before heading out the door, because if there's one thing he's learned about the weather, it's that a storm front can cross the entire Midwest faster than a meteorologist can grab a cup of coffee during a quick commercial break.

My father-in-law has abided by this plan for the four-teen years that we have lived within driving range. Not once has he deviated from the plan. Not once has the plan been subject to change or flexibility.

We tried making a few plans for my father-in-law once. After he had been a widower for a year, we began making subtle suggestions that he consider selling the place and move into one of those nice retirement villages where the lawn maintenance is taken care of for you and ducks swim in a man-made lake. We even suggested that he might move closer to us. At the very least, we hoped he would be amenable to our plan that he eat more fresh fruits and vegetables and lay off all the bacon and sausage.

We threw out a multitude of good plans and he ignored them all. He waited until the family was together and announced that after serious thought, he had made a plan of his own.

His plan was to buy a brand new convertible. He'd

always wanted one and he thought that age eighty-seven was as good a time as any. We took turns staggering to the bathroom to splash cold water on our faces.

"Be practical!" we howled in unison.

Practical? He pointed out that he wasn't exactly living the lifestyle of the rich and famous. He was still on that small acreage in the old farmhouse that had been in the family for nearly a century. He saved empty margarine tubs, rarely bought more than four green bananas at a time, and always shopped with coupons. He had lived a lifetime of practical. Practical shoes. Practical station wagons. Practical sedans.

"Please, please be practical!" we continued wailing.

He ignored us. He tuned out the caterwauling and began thinking to himself.

Over and over the same thought kept coming to his mind: Chevy. The thought grew clearer: Chevy Cavalier. He continued thinking. White. Yes, white would be his first choice. Dark blue if the dealer couldn't get white. Actually, it was more of an azure than a dark blue, at least that's the way it looked in the color brochure hidden beneath his stack of *National Geographic*s and *Reader's Digest*s on the end table.

"It's not safe," said my sister-in-law, stomping her foot as she hit the word safe.

"How practical is it to buy a convertible and then have it stolen? Is that what you want?"

He thought for our combined intelligence and college educations, that at least one of us would have heard of the anti-theft device known as The Club. Of course he wouldn't want his convertible stolen. He wouldn't want his hip broken either, but that didn't mean he'd stay in bed all day.

"Is it a practical move—financially?" inquired another loved one.

He'd worked with numbers all his life and now he was being asked if he knew how to add and subtract from his bank account. A loud thud vibrated beneath a pair of shoes as an emotionally distraught family member slumped to the floor in distress.

My father-in-law was deep in thought and we knew it. For a moment we backed off. Perhaps at last he was thinking sensibly. Little did we know, he *was* thinking sensibly—about the pros and cons of cruise control and an adjustable tilt steering wheel.

"How much would you even drive it?" demanded yet another caring soul.

"Probably just during nice weather," he said patiently. Then again, maybe he'd pick up Marvin and Virginia and Carmen and they'd loop the city with the top down and the radio blaring in the middle of December with icy snowflakes stinging their faces. Maybe he'd drive it every day of the year, half an hour before sunset, just to see the sky fade to orange and to feel the wind ripple through every strand of hair he had left.

"This needs a lot of thought, doesn't it?" someone asked in that tone of voice parents use to remind young children to wash their hands after using the potty.

He nodded his head and agreed that we were right. It *did* require a lot of thought. Which was why the first thing the next morning he headed to a car dealer west of town. This was a far larger dealership than the two he had been to the day before. A bigger dealer could well mean lower prices. After all, it was the practical thing to do.

And my mother wants to know what plans we have for our aging parents? What plans do we have for two hyperactive grandparents with more zest for life than most Baby Boomers half their age? What plans do we have for my octogenarian father-in-law with a sharp car and and an even sharper memory? Mom's really slipping if she thinks I don't recognize a trick question when I see it.

46

Greater Than

As a small child, there were three things I thought I would never master: chewing with my mouth shut, sitting with my knees together, and being certain of whether the arrow in math class pointing to the right meant greater than or less than.

Chewing with my mouth shut became a lot easier once all my permanent teeth arrived. Today, I am a reasonably polite dinner partner, providing there are no cherry tomatoes in the salad.

Sitting ladylike in a dress became easier once my pudgy little legs began to grow and my feet could finally touch the floor. I have also come to effortlessly recognize that the caret pointed to the right, >, means greater than. It's such a handy symbol that I've adopted it into my note taking. The list of things I have to do by Friday is > the time I have to do them in. The number of calories I have taken in today is > the number of calories I have burned.

Despite such flawless mastery, the > continues to deal me fits. Let me explain.

For generations, Greek men traditionally carried worry beads in their pockets. These were small, colorful beads on a string, or precious gemstones strung on a chain. When confronted with a problem, taken by surprise, or faced with unwelcome news, men would stroke their beards with one hand and finger worry beads with the other. Over time, the worry beads would become worn and smooth or, in the case of easily agitated men with an extremely low tolerance for stress, completely worn out.

The concept of worry beads is appealing. But being that I am neither Greek, nor male, nor heavily bearded, the concept also presents certain limitations. Actually, the main problem is that I am female, which means I can't depend on my pants having pockets in which to carry worry beads.

The contemporary American counterpart to worry beads would be stress balls, those squishy plastic balls that look like miniature porcupines without heads. Another fine coping technique to be sure, but a little too obvious. Bouncing a stress ball from palm to palm in public doesn't exactly give off a "You-can-count-on-me-I'm-a-dependable-sort" kind of message. It gives off more of "I-just-escaped-two-days-ago-and-they-are-looking-for-me-as-we-speak" kind of air.

As a compromise, I've tried to imagine I have one of those greater than (>) math signs in my pocket. An invisible reminder that, in spite of all the worries and dilemmas of everyday life, God is greater than....

But, try as I might, I easily forget. I forget that God is greater than the insurance premium for two teenage drivers. I forget that God is greater than that chirping sound the refrigerator is making. I fail to remember that He is greater than this morning's heated argument with the better half. I outright panic when I loose sight that God is even greater than diabetes, cancer, or Alzheimer's.

As Americans, our lives have never been easier, yet stress has never been more epidemic. Speculation abounds that life in the fast lane is paving the way for the Age of Melancholy. The World Health Organization calculates that depression is on the way to becoming the world's second most disabling disease in the next decade. Today, we have a virtual smorgasbord of depression: adult depression, adolescent depression, holiday depression, seasonal light-deprivation depression, post-partum depression, and senior citizen depression. We're so depressed that even our dogs are depressed.

Abraham Lincoln used the phrase "black dog" to describe his ongoing struggle with stress and depression. Shakespeare wrote that hope is sometimes the only medicine that the miserable have. In recent years, many members of the medical community have given Shakespeare a mighty Amen.

Several years ago, one thousand doctors, nurses, and other health professionals worldwide registered for a first-of-its-kind event at the Harvard Medical School—a conference designed to teach the value of prayer and other spiritual pursuits as healing tools. One of the event organizers and professors involved with the event said that some religious influences are "the mental equivalent of nuclear energy."

Hundreds of studies have found that prayer and faith cause specific physiological changes that resemble relaxation. They found that people who attend religious services are more likely to have sound moral judgment; more likely to have children who exercise sexual restraint; more likely to possess family and marital happiness.

The greatest thing about all these findings—in a world where treating stress has become a national pastime, a daytime talk show obsession, and a billion-dollar industry—is that these treatments are absolutely free. No appointment needed, no special training required, no therapy advised. Sometimes the cure for stress can be as simple as sliding into a pew, showing up for temple, opening a Bible to the Psalms, reading the Gospels, or bringing to mind that little mathematical symbol and remembering that God *is* greater than.

Epilogue

The book of Ecclesiastes says there is a time for every thing and a season for every activity under heaven. A time to be born. A time to die. A time to laugh. A time to weep.

Life is an ever-changing mix of seasons. Joy kisses us on one cheek while sorrow plants a big, sloppy, wet one on the other. Stress is a season that knows no boundaries. Stress does not discriminate based on race, age, sex, finances, modem speeds, weather forecasts, or major holidays.

The author of Ecclesiastes, King Solomon, was one of those guys who, as we say today, had it all: intelligence, money, power, and camels. And then one day, it all started to slowly unravel. Solomon's writing reveals a man all stressed up with no place to go. Ecclesiastes reads like he's wandering through stacks of self-improvement books, searching and searching for the antidote to a heavy and dreary life. He explores fulfillment through philosophy, fine architecture, gardening, cattle breeding (please tell me that one won't cycle around again anytime soon), art collecting, religious rituals, and wealth.

As a kindred spirit often caught in a wrestling match with stress, I offer the following update on the seasons of life with sincere apologies to King Solomon—and with a quiet confidence that he would entirely understand.

There is an appointed time for everything.
And there is a time for every stress under heaven—

A time to panic and a time to pray,

A time to breathe deep and a time to hyperventilate
into a brown paper bag,

A time to cry and a time to reapply mascara
and pull yourself together,

A time to hurry and a time to sit
quietly beneath the stars,

A time to multi-task and a time to
refrain from all things taxing,

A time to volunteer and a time
to not answer the phone,

A time to gripe and a time to be grateful,

A time to let out a primal scream and
a time to hold your tongue,

A time to worry and pace the floor and a
time to forget about it and go to bed,

A time for herbal therapy and
a time for estrogen,

*A time to do aerobics and a time to
return to the buffet,*

*A time to pursue perfection and a time when
"good enough" will do just fine,*

*A time to unclutter and a time to let
it all pile up in a corner,*

*A time to strive to understand the opposite sex
and a time to believe in mysteries.*

Oh yes, one more thing. Solomon finally comes to a place of rest at the end of Ecclesiastes. He offers a solution that, along with liberal doses of chocolate and occasional afternoons in a hammock, works wonders in taming stress:

*"Fear God and keep His commandments;
for this is the whole duty of man."*

About the Author

Charlie Nye

Lori Borgman's humor column on parenting and family life is nationally distributed by Knight Ridder Information News Service. She has worked as a photojournalist and a news editor and has racked up a few journalism awards along the way, but her greatest honor is hearing a reader say, "I have one of your columns hanging on my fridge."

She lives with her family in Indianapolis where she and her husband often spend Friday nights sitting on the couch, all stressed up with no place to go. She is also the author of *Pass the Faith, Please* and *I Was a Better Mother Before I Had Kids*.

If you would like information regarding having Lori Borgman as a speaker for your group or organization, e-mail Lori directly at lori@loriborgman.com or contact her agent, Bob Cassidy of Cassidy and Fishman, at (508) 485-8996 or speakers@cassidyandfishman.com

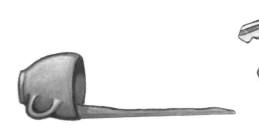

I Was a Better Mother Before I Had Kids

by Lori Borgman

"Borgman will make parents laugh out loud or bring tears to their eyes..."
— PUBLISHERS WEEKLY

Once, Lori Borgman had parenting all figured out. Her cheerfully compliant children would play peacefully in a tidy yard, happily snack on fruit and whole wheat bread, and implore her to read Longfellow aloud as they drift off for a welcome nap.

That was *before* she had kids—kids who stand up in their highchairs. Shove peas up their noses. Throw pre-nap tantrums, all in quadraphonic stereo sound....

I Was a Better Mother Before I Had Kids is Lori Borgman's fuzzy and prickly ode to parenthood, a laugh-out-loud reality check that only a seasoned mother of three could write. Drawn from her wildly popular newspaper columns, these wise and witty snapshots capture family life as it really is—part Norman Rockwell, part Stephen King—and where *nothing* is as Lori Borgman imagined it would be in her pre-baby days.

In league with Dave Barry, Erma Bombeck, and Anna Quindlen, but with a voice uniquely her own, Lori Borgman plunges into parenthood with her eyes wide open, and laughs along with us at the perils—er, make that the joys—of family life.

Price $14.99 Paperback
ISBN: 1-57860-213-0

To order call: 1(800)343-4499 www.emmisbooks.com
Emmis Books 1700 Madison Road Cincinnati, Ohio 45206

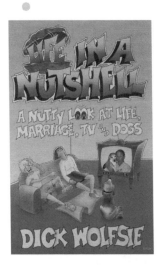

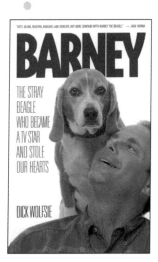

Barney
The Stray Beagle Who Became a TV Star and Stole Our Hearts
by Dick Wolfsie

The greatest Barney moments, told by his faithful human sidekick—a book destined to make dog lovers laugh, cry, and howl at the moon.

Running out the door one very cold morning, TV reporter Dick Wolfsie nearly tripped over a tiny beagle on his front step. In his haste, he welcomed the little stray into the house and rushed off to work.

Eight hours later, Dick returned to a shredded couch, a well-gnawed pair of heels, mangled curtains, and a damp rug. Dick's wife issued an ultimatum: "The dog must go. Either that, or you have to take him to work with you."

From this humble beginning, a star was born. Barney the Beagle's career in the public eye included 3,000 shows, 14 commercials, and 12 straight years on the air. And when Barney died, Dick received 1,700 emails and letters expressing sympathy and condolences.

If you followed Barney's antics over the years, you'll recognize your favorite Barney stories here, plus more than a few surprises. If you missed Barney on TV, here's your chance to meet an unforgettable beagle who had heart, brains, and moxie to spare.

Price $14.99 Paperback
ISBN: 1-57860-167-3

To order call: 1(800)343-4499 www.emmisbooks.com
Emmis Books 1700 Madison Road Cincinnati, Ohio 45206